To my wonderful
friend Clare
Thank you for
Being a part
of it all.
Love
D.W. Smoth

Love, Hate, Deceit, and Foul Play in the Afternoon

A Two Act Comedy

by
D. M. Schuetteé

authorHOUSE™

1663 LIBERTY DRIVE, SUITE 200
BLOOMINGTON, INDIANA 47403
(800) 839-8640
WWW.AUTHORHOUSE.COM

First published by AuthorHouse 05/17/05

ISBN: 1-4208-3529-7 (sc)

Printed in the United States of America
Bloomington, Indiana

This book is printed on acid-free paper.

Some times in life you come across some extraordinary people, that hang on to you no matter what, those wonderful people are my friends, who I adore and treasure with all my heart a special thank you goes out them.

Mom & Dad: Thank you for all your love, and support to my creativity. Love you both!

Michael: Thank you for the awesome times at Fremont Experience Love Ya Bro.

Tim: Thank you for the fun times when we all get together to go out fishing! Love Ya Bro.

Tracy Tabin Thank you for letting me sit at your computer to re-type and re-write this show,
On those Saturday mornings, and how I would read aloud the dialog and say…"Is that funny? Or should I change it? *"I got your Coffee"*

Bill Tomasini Thank you for that wonderful night long ago, when we all sat around in your living room reading the play and hearing all the wonderful voices that brought life to the show.
Thank you for being a part of it all

Clare Terrill Thank you for giving the character Lillian a voice, and thank you for taking on the wheels every night. And I can't forget the first one on the scene to take on the daunting task as you started using that little bright red pen of yours to edit the script.

Paul Boisvert Thank you for that Sunday at your house that we sat at your kitchen table laughing as you acted out some of the scenes in the show. And of course, giving it another editing face-lift. How could I forget those long fabulous bike rides. I couldn't have done it without you.
Yvon Blackburn Thank you, you were always there to lend a helping hand and there in the audience every night supporting, the cast buying refreshments when we were all starving at rehearsals. Thanks you Frenchie

Ron Gibson Thank you, so much for getting the approval from the board and getting in there with your awesome directing skills to give the show a chance to been seen and heard on stage.

Rosemary Gibson Thank you for your great artistic insight to the show, and having fun in the role of Audrey! I must say a true trooper! *"Boy those damn crutches"*

Carolyn Lori Thank you, who drove nine hours and then some to hear the show what a fabulous fun time we all had down town in Sacramento. *"Carolyn that way, no down town is that way. Love ya!*

David Lori Thank you for lending your excellent building skills to the set and of course of being an important part of the theatre family. Thank you!

Gil Carrillo Thank you, who saw that surprising performance of "the Dying Gaul and how we would talk for hours about the show. Who could forget spending our Friday afternoons with Music in the Park Yeah!

The cast of: Love, hate, deceit and foul play... All those rehearsal nights I sat in the audience laughing my ass off. Thank you!

The Santa Maria Theatre Board of Directors Thank you for voting the show in.
Thank you attending the performances Thank you everyone for a terrific experience!

The lambda Players in Sacramento, thank you Clint, for giving this show another reading Performance!

Susan, Melanie, and all the wonderful staff at Emerald Suites: who help keep the place alive and well!

Loving you always,

D.M.SCHUETTEE'

I would like to dedicate this show to my loving family:
Dysfunctional, and some times a little insane,
I wouldn't have them any other way.

Notes about the show

Between the acts during your intermission time

There should be sounds of television commercials playing over your sound system as the house lights come up.

<u>Theatres</u>

You may create some television commercials yourself
To give the Illusion to the show that we the audience are watching a television show.

<u>One final note:</u>

This show may also be performed
as an illusion of one of those reality TV shows

Introduction

It was in the winter of 1991, I was at home in my little one bedroom apartment in California, and I was working for Hughes Aircraft at the time. I just finished my shift at work, raced out of the parking lot drove down on Carmen Ave. whipped around the corner and pulled my little black Volkswagen rabbit up to the front curb of the apartment complex. Raced inside at apoxicamly12: 35 am frantically looking for my writing tablet to jot down my wonderful play idea that had been brewing in my head all day.

I quickly sat down at the kitchen table where my pen couldn't keep up with my thoughts. My ideas poured out like a glass of spilled milk. Then they stop at 2:40 in morning. I closed the tablet and went to bed. But sleep eluded me as the thoughts came back. I had to write all my ideas down quickly, all of them before they drove me nuts. Some times that happens to playwrights when thoughts come in hoards, well for me any way.

There it was the very first rough draft on paper in front of me with no title. Damn!

So, I let my thoughts out, but nothing not a clear thought in sight. I even relaxed to have something come to me. Nothing...Damn!

So, I knew the very thing that would help me, I drove to the beach on my day off.

I strolled down along the shoreline with the wet sand between my toes and still nothing.

What was wrong with me, it was a beautiful day, in fact a gorgeous day, but still no tittle for my Play. Well then I tried another thing; I went down town to the mall. Oh yes the mall, hey there has to be a title there some where amongst all those window shoppers and families eating ice cream huh? But with the entire meaningless walking window shopping zombies, I was still no closer to having a title for the play.

Then three days went by, I was just about to fall asleep on the sofa, when it hit me like a heavy sandbag during a flood. Those three days where just enough to feed my thoughts.

On the day at the beach I took the afternoon to stroll down the sand, Hmm Afternoon, OK. There was a word.

Then one foggy day, I heard through those paper thin walls, sitting on the couch in my apartment, my next door neighbor, who can't hear has to have his television volume level at 102, at some show on with some god awful day time soap. That's it, that was all I needed, Yeah! All I needed was a little "Love, Hate, deceit, and foul play in the afternoon"

D.M. SHUETTEE'

"Love Hate Deceit & Foul Play in the Afternoon"

Was first produced on December 19, 1998 at the Santa Maria Civic Theatre Workshop
Santa Maria California

Directed and Set Designed by Ron Gibson, Stage Manager, Carolyn Taylor

Francis Bovell..Miles Greenup

Mason Bovell...Danny Maher

Susan O'Nelly..Catherine Brown

Antoine Devinio..Leo Cortez

Lillian Bovell...Clare Terrill

Audrey Van Lorinsen.................................Rosemary Gibson

Nina Chadwell..Jill Zadar

Eli Chamber...Michael Brockelhurst

Characters

Francis Bovell
A handsome, 30-year-old, daytime soap star, on the daytime drama "As the Evening Falls"

Mason Bovell
Brother to Francis, also in his 30's a writer for the show "As the Evening Falls"

Susan O'Nelly
Lillian's live-in personal Assistant

Antoine Devinio
Live-in domestic to Lillian

Lillian Bovell
An elegant woman of her sixties, retired, former talk show host

Audrey Van Lorinsen
A woman in her late forties, divorced, Lillian's sister

Nina Chadwell
Lillian's neighbor, a gossip columnist for the "Hollywood Informer"

Eli Chambers
Lillian's gardener, a gentleman in his late 40's

ACT 1

Place: San Francisco, California
The Time: 1:45am Saturday, the present
The setting: *The residence of Lillian Bovell, a very elegantly styled San Francisco home that overlooks the city. USL is the front door to the house with a Roman style archway over the door. From the front entry is a hallway that leads to other rooms in the house. From the hallway DSR is a door that leads into Lillian's room. Directly next to her room DSR is a wooden desk with a chair, where letters and other mail are placed.*

Also DSR is a door which is the downstairs bathroom, USR in the corner of the room, is a bay window with a window seat. This window overlooks the San Francisco Bay. USC with the same Roman style archway with columns to support the structure is an elegant staircase with pictures that follow up the stairway leading to other rooms in the house. Two fichus trees stand as soldiers next to the columns. Directly to one side of the staircase is a small round table on which a medium size vase sits. SL are French doors, foliage plants, and flowers are visible on the path that leads to the outside garden. From the French doors you can see an outside setting with flower urns and a garden bench to represent the outside of the house. DSC is the sofa and end tables. Underneath the sofa is a designer rug. To one side of the sofa is the television, on top of a rectangular table. Finally on both sides of the stage, left and right are two French providential chairs. The scene is dark; moonlight pierces through the French doors.

At rise: *There are sounds of crickets and a dog barking in the distance. Voices are heard off stage. A few moments pass, then Francis and Mason, both handsome young men in their 30's enter. Both are well dressed and wearing overcoats. They soon pass the French doors outside. A sound of a tree branch snaps.*

Francis
Shhh! (*Another sound of a tree branch snapping*). Quiet, Mason!

Mason
Sorry

Francis
What are you doing?

1

Mason
Nothing, why?

Francis
You're making enough noise to wake all of San Francisco.

Mason
Francis, why don't we just call mama on the cell phone? That should be a surprise enough. We haven't seen her since she moved here.

Francis
Mason, we do call her, but we never gave her a surprise visit, and tonight's the night.

Mason
Listen, Francis, I don't think this is a good idea. Why do we have to give mother a surprise visit? Surprising her like this, might give her a stroke for God sakes. Why didn't you let her know we're coming, she would've liked that. Why go through all the trouble with this stupid surprise crap?

Francis
Shhh quiet!

Mason
This is stupid. (*He walks toward him and trips*). Ahh shit!

Francis
Mason, you're going to wake the whole neighborhood, and ruin our plan!

Mason
Hell what do you want me to do, it's dark out here!

Francis
Watch where you're going! (*Susan enters from her room upstairs and goes into the kitchen*).

Mason
I think my knee is swelling.

Francis
Oh get real

Mason
It is!

Francis
How do you know, you said you can't see, it's dark out here, remember?

Mason
I can feel my own knee.

Francis
Keep quiet, come over here and sit down.

(Antoine enters from his upstairs room and goes to the bathroom).

Francis
Uh oh.

Mason
Uh oh what?

Francis
I don't have the key.

Mason
What?

Francis
I said I don't have the key.

Mason
Smooth move exlax! I can't believe this!!

Francis
Shhh! What did I say about the noise level? Shhh!

Mason
Oh shh, shhh yourself! I knew this was a bad idea. Cop comes patrolling by, sees us, we're in jail... Oh won't that make a wonderful story for the tabloids, Soap star Bovell in jail for breaking and entering his own mother's house, because he just wanted to give her a surprise visit.

Francis
Keep it down! You're going to blow it for us!

Mason
I should have called; I have to be a fool to listen to you.

Francis
You are. You have the key?

Mason
Me?

Francis
No, one of the next door neighbors!

Mason
If I had it, I would have given it to you by now. Why would I have it?
I didn't come up with this crazy idea in the first place. A surprise
visit, Ha! If it would have been my idea, I would have planned,
packed a few things, dressed for the occasion, set the schedule,
thought it out logically.

Francis
Stop your damn complaining. Do you want cheese with that whine?

(Francis starts off).

Mason
Where are you going?

Francis
I'm going to check in the car.

Mason
For what?

Francis
For the key, Mr. Logic!

Mason
Francis, just knock on the door.

Francis
And ruin the surprise?

Mason
(Mimicking) And ruin the surprise.

Francis
Stay there, and don't you dare knock!

Mason
Francis I have one word...Difficult!

(Susan exits from the kitchen, then starts back to her room, then Antoine exits from the bathroom and walks to the kitchen, then Susan exits from her room and enters the bathroom, then from outside car lights flash by the French doors and Mason ducks to avoid the lights but falls down in the process., Francis returns to Mason).

Francis
(Calling out). Mason! Mason. *(He walks about).* Mason where are you? *(Stepping on his brother).*

Mason
Ouch! Hey! Watch it!

Francis
What are you doing on the ground?

Mason
I tripped.

Francis
I told you to watch where you're going...Now be quiet and follow me.

(They walk to the French doors and jiggle the handle, and whisper to each other. Antoine re-enters, stops, hears the noise from the two, and freezes in his tracks in a panic, then he runs into the kitchen).

Mason
Are you sure that's the right key.

Francis
Yes, I'm sure.

Mason
Then why isn't the door open?

Francis
I don't know.

Mason
Has it ever occurred to you that you might have the wrong key?

Francis
Mason please, just please shut up and let me think.

(Again they whisper among themselves from outside. Susan exits from the bathroom and sees the two men silhouetted against the French doors, and she dashes for the telephone but it is too far for her to make the

9-11 call. As the two men enter she makes a mad dash in front of the sofa. The two men fumble about, Antoine sneaks in with a spatula in his hand, and hides by the high back chair).

Francis
Quiet, and don't make any noise this ought to be a surprise.

Mason
And what a surprise

(There is a noise from Susan).

Mason
I heard something.

Francis
Get the flashlight!

Mason
What flashlight? We didn't bring a flashlight.

Francis
Shit, shit, shit!

Mason
Shhh, shhh, shhh!

Francis
(He stands at the French doors).

Hey who's in here!

Mason
Like they would tell you.

Francis
I have to find the lights *(He panics and starts for the lights).*

Mason
No! Don't go in there!

(Antoine in a panic leaps on Mason's back, hitting him with a spatula. MASON YELLS).

Mason
Help!

(Susan is now in the muck of things and defends herself, by attacking Francis from behind).

Francis
No help me!

Susan
Back off buddy, or I'll scream!

Antoine
If she doesn't, I will!

(By now, all are wrestling on the living room floor. Then suddenly the lights come on and Lillian and elegant French woman appears sitting in a wheelchair somewhat fragile wearing her house robe, she appears startled by the surprise visit. Standing up in the middle of the room is Susan, a pretty young girl in her 20's, dressed in her house robe and slippers. Antoine picks himself up off the floor. He is an attractive young man in his late 20's. He is dressed in jockey shorts and a ribbed tank top. They all focus on Francis and Mason).

Lillian
My God what's going on…Mason, Francis?

Mason
Ma'Ma!

Francis
Hi Ma'Ma…Ma'Ma what happened to you?

(At this moment off stage sounds of whimpering. Everyone turns looking for the source of the noise, then the noise becomes louder and louder. Lillian's sister, Audrey in her 40's, crawls down the stairs

7

wearing a designer Muumuu, curlers in her hair, cream covering her face and a bandage around her foot, supported by two crutches. She whimpers as she takes each step down the stairs. This freezes the action. The brother's look about for the source of the whimpering).

Mason
(Looking about).
What's that?

Antoine
The Anti-Christ.

Audrey
(Audrey, comes crawling down the stairs, squinting her eyes) Stand back Lillian, I'm here to protect you!

Lillian
Oh no.

Antoine
Oh yes.

Susan
(Extending her arm as a welcome to Audrey) Here she comes.

Mason
(Noticing) Auntie Audrey?

Susan
Here we go again.

Lillian
Audrey, put the crutch down.

Antoine
She's too much for words.

Susan
Uh huh.

Lillian
Audrey careful! *(her French sets in under stress)* Faites Attention!

(Audrey swings the crutch, coming too close to the small vase on the table)

Audrey
Stand back you! And you too mister!

Lillian
Pour l'amour Dieu! Audrey!

Susan
Ah a touch of French, oui.

Audrey
Don't come any closer, or you're going down!

Lillian
Audrey! Audrey! *(Audrey swings the crutch back and forth as a weapon)*

Antoine
It's too late; she's in her police dog attack mode. *(Audrey, finally smashes the vase to the floor)*

Susan
She broke another one.

Lillian
Thank God it wasn't a motif. Audrey, Audrey listen to me! Put the crutch down!

(Audrey does & fumbles and falls to the ground, while the others watch with pain)

Oh, that's gonna leave a big purple mark. Mason and Francis gave us a surprise visit.

Audrey
Mason and Francis here? I don't have my glasses on. It's hard to make out people

when I don't have them on.

Lillian
(Sarcastically) Really, do you think so?

Audrey
Gosh, Francis, Mason, you're both here. Wow how exciting. It's been awhile. *(She notices the broken vase)*

9

Oh Lilly dear I'm sorry, I didn't mean to break that vase.

Antoine
Or the other two, you broke yesterday.

Audrey
(To Antoine) I was startled and I heard screams and a lot of noise, I
was trying to protect you.

Lillian
Audrey, you don't have to explain, just please no more broken vases.
Besides dear,

(Turning to her two sons) Mason and Francis will take care of it.
Surprise!

Mason
(Giving her a hug) Ma'Ma, sorry about all of this. I don't know
what we were thinking. We didn't mean to scare you. *(Taking notice
of her in a wheelchair)*

What happened, why are you in a wheelchair?

Lillian
I'll tell you in a minute. Now what is this all about? But first we
need to help Audrey up off of the floor.

(The two sons help Audrey up off the floor)

Francis
Audrey, please forgive us for scaring you out of your wits.

Audrey
Well I heard all this commotion, so I thought that I needed to protect
her. What else could I do?

Susan
Stop watching that show "Cops."

Audrey
I'll be all right, just help me to the sofa. What a klutz I am…that
was some scare we got from you two.

10

Francis
Well sneaking in and all, I really didn't think this would happen.
(Mason gives Francis a look).

Lillian
Now what's all this sneaking in business, and how did you two get in?

Mason
It was Francis's idea, him and his secret decoder ring. Tell her, Francis.

Lillian
Yes, tell me, Francis

Francis
I kept the key the last time we were here, Ma'Ma. *(As he gives her a hug to butter her up).* Sorry to upset things, stupid idea huh? Well since the both of us have time off, and since Mason nearly has next week's show all written and ready to go, and we haven't seen you since you moved here to the city, we wanted to spend some tine visiting, some catching up to do. We... *(Mason clears his throat).* I wanted to give you a surprise visit...are you surprised?

Lillian
Terribly.

Francis
Susan, that was you, who grabbed me? *(Realizing he was wrestling with her).* Oh I'm so sorry are you okay?

Susan
I'm okay that scared the jaheebies out of me *(She's mesmerized by seeing him, here in her presence).*

Francis
You handle yourself very well I wouldn't want to tangle with you again. Are you sure you're all right?

Susan
I'm alright. Sorry to stare. Wow you're here. . . . *(She continues to stare at Francis).* I watch the show religiously. It's my favorite soap. I love your character Cameron. Excuse me. . .it's that you're even sexier in person. You smell nice...I mean. Yeah, well you know

11

what I mean. *(Still in awe of Francis)*.

Antoine
What she's trying to say is that she doesn't get out much...Oh my head. *(He sits down on the sofa)*.

Lillian
Antoine, are you all right?

Mason
Did I do that? *(Antoine moans)*. I'm sorry. *(He moans again)*. I'm terribly sorry.

Lillian
What sons I have. You two sneak in here, cause havoc, and beat up my help. What kind of visit is this?

Antoine
I better get this mess cleaned up, and get some ice on my head.

Mason
Let me help. It's too late to mention this but, I think, if one of us had turned on the lights, maybe all this wouldn't have happened.

Susan
Yeah you're right, I couldn't get to them in time, and there is all this construction going in the city to improve earthquake safety, it seems like to me San Francisco, is always under construction.

Francis
Ma'Ma now, enough about us please tell us what happened to you?

Mason
Was it a dog?

Lillian
No it wasn't a dog.

Mason
Was it a cop?

Audrey
It could happen.

Lillian
I did it on the kitchen floor.

Mason
Oooh hot date huh?

Lillian
Let me clarify it for you. The accident happened in the kitchen
on the floor. Antoine was cooking, he accidentally spilled a pot of
noodles, and I slipped on them, I fractured my hip.

Mason
(To Antoine) Maybe you were cooking with too much olive oil; any
cooking oil is going to be slippery.

Lillian
(Changing the subject) But the bone is healing just fine.

Mason
Francis, feel better now about your friggin surprise visit?

Francis
I admit you were right.

Mason
Next time listen to your younger brother, make the call. *(Antoine re-
enters with dust pan and broom to clean up the broken vase).* Ma'Ma,
will you be able to back to work?

Lillian
Sweetie, I don't know if I told you, I retired last year from the show.

Francis
What?

Lillian
I figured it was time to go. Besides … The ratings were down.

Mason
Now that you're not working, how do you manage?

Lillian
I manage just fine, with Susan here. Of course, she's been with me
since Moses was a child. A true saint she is. Antoine came aboard
last year and has adapted wonderfully to a bunch of mixed nuts.

13

They both have been great help to me.

Audrey

Lil, I try to do my best, to do my share around here, but tonight it doesn't show. I shouldn't have stayed this long. Don't worry it won't be long before I'm back home and things will be normal for you again.

Lillian

Now Audrey, I didn't mean it that way. Every one has different circumstances in their lives. I understand yours.

Antoine

I'm glad some one does.

Francis

Audrey, what happened to you, did you slip in the kitchen on the oily noodles too?

Antoine

I'm glad someone does.

Francis

Audrey, what happened to you, did you slip in the kitchen on the wet noodles?

Antoine

Here we go again.

Audrey

You mean my foot? I did it by jumping out of a dumpster.

Francis

What were you doing in a dumpster? You didn't loose your job did you?

Audrey

Oh no, Cheeto, my cat ran down the back alley near the house. Poor thing hasn't been fixed yet. I was sure I put that in my daily planner to have that done. He's always playing with other cats, ya' know, playing or being chased by my friend's dog Pee-Pee. So I went to look for him. Then I found him in a dumpster, once in there he couldn't get out, so I crawled inside to get the poor dear.

Just as I was about to jump out of a dumpster Mr. Carmen, me next door neighbor, out of all people, saw me and the jerk asked it I was eating out.

Mason
(Concerned). Were you?

Audrey
No. Anyway as I jumped out of the dumpster, I sprained my foot and poor Cheeto scratched me. I'm stuck here for awhile until those nasty creatures are finished being exterminated.

Francis
What kind of creatures.

Audrey
(Obviously lying). Uh..Termites.

Francis
You have termites in your house?

Antoine
And bats in her belfry.

Susan
Amen.

Lillian
So now that is out of the way. How long do you plan to visit?

Francis
(Jokingly). For about three days.

Lillian
Three? And you scared the shit out of us! For that! Excuse my French.

Francis
Whoa, I was just kidding. You don't mind it it's for a couple of weeks?

Lillian
I don't know. After what you caused tonight, you should go bungee jumping in the nude!

Mason
I'll alert the media.

Susan
Francis, I know this might sound silly. I wanted to ask you the last time I saw you. . . I don't know if I should, nah it's silly.

Francis
No go ahead ask me.

Susan
Its teenager stuff.

Francis
Ask me!

Susan
Is it possible for me to get your autograph?

Francis
Better yet, I'll sign a photo of me.

Mason
He has a whole suitcase full. *(Francis walks outside of the French doors to retrieve his briefcase).*

Audrey
Mason, I've been wanting to ask you, on the show is Ashley Steele going to die soon?

Antoine
She doesn't, does she? I hope not, I love her.

Mason
I shouldn't tell you...OK don't say anything to anyone. The producers want me to keep her in.

Audrey
No. After what she's done to her sister and her husband, not to mention the dog. She's a sadistic bitch.

Antoine
And a good one too.

Susan
Francis she's not the one that Cameron marries, is she?

Francis
Well I can't say. It's hush hush. *(He starts to sign his photograph of himself for Susan).*

Lillian
That reminds me. With all the noise you two have made, I hope Nina wasn't up next door. That little busy body, always conjuring up ideas to write Trashy stories for the Hollywood Informer. She became head columnist last year for that rag.

Francis
That's all I need. *(He goes to close the curtains).*

Mason
You live next door to a tabloid columnist? They're not writers they're vultures preying on the famous.

Lillian
That's definitely true. Last year after she became somewhat of a friend, I was forced to threaten to sue her for writing an awful story about me. But I wouldn't give her the opportunity, if you know what I mean. Well you better bring in your things quietly.

Mason
Well nice friendship you have going there. You amaze me still living on the edge with people.

Francis
Now where was I? *(As he is signing the photo).*

Susan
Well, we can start with my name.

Francis
Right. *(Having fun with her).* That's always a start.

Mason
Francis!

Francis
In a minute.

Mason
I need help bring in <u>your</u> things.

Antoine
(Offering). I'll help.

Mason
Antoine, right? I look pretty bad tonight in front of everybody.
That's the last time I listen to my brother. I couldn't ask you to help
after all this business of sneaking in scaring everyone. It's all right I
can handle this.

Susan
(She looks at the signed photo). Wow, thank you.

Francis
Anytime.

Mason
Oh forget it, Francis!

Susan
I think your brother is angry.

Francis
He's a temperamental writer, can snap any moment.

Antoine
Here, let me.

Mason
Are you sure you don't mind.

(He opens the door).

Antoine
Believe me I don't mind, you're cute.

Mason
(Taken by surprise by his comment). Uh…uh…unlike my brother, I
don't have a photograph of me to sign for you. I'm just a writer, he's
the star.

Antoine
(Seeing the car).

Its okay I like writer, they're so poetic. Wow, a Lamborghini. Never drove in one of those. How about a ride?

Mason
It belongs to Francis...*(Going for it)*. Why not, sure let's go for a ride. *(They exit out the front door)*.

Susan
(She starts up the stairs). I better go get blankets and pillows for you two.

Francis
Here let me help you. *(They exit, Music starts)*.

Lillian
Audrey, I wonder why they didn't call first.

Audrey
Beats the hell out of me.

(Black out).

ACT 1

Scene 2

(Early morning, the door bell rings, Susan's voice is heard off stage).

Susan
Antoine! Antoine! *(The door bell continues to ring)*. Hold onto your bloomers!...Antoine where are you?

Antoine
Susan I would get the door, but I'm on the throne.

Susan
(She looks through the peephole of the front door, she sees Nina the next door neighbor).
Oh no. Not now.

Antoine
Susan who is it?

19

Susan
It's Nina.

Antoine
Tell her we don't have her broom!

Susan
(She opens the door. Standing in the doorway is Nina. Early fifties dressed in black spandex pants, long black velvet blouse. A wide black brim hat and eye glasses that sit on the edge of her nose... She snoops about in the doorway as if she is getting the next scoop on a story for the papers). Morning, Nina.

Nina
Hello Susan and how are you this morning?

Susan
A little tired.

Nina
Oh really, why?

Susan
I just couldn't sleep, I was up all night *(Covering)*, I mean out. I was out all night.

Nina
Uh huh. I went out in my backyard and picked some apples off of my tree, I thought Lillian might like some.

Susan
That's nice of you, I'm sure she would appreciate them. Talk to you later.

(Attempting to close the door).

Nina
Not leaving yet deary. Whose Lamborghini is parked in front of the house?

Susan
(Looking out the front door). That one?

Nina
Yes that one.

Susan
(Thinking to cover). I believe, it belongs to…to…

Nina
To whom?

Susan
It's the neighbors. You know the guy who lives across from us.

Nina
Barry, the hairstylist? I know he doesn't have a Lamborghini. He owns a 63 Volkswagen bug.

Susan
Maybe he got a raise.

Nina
And I'm a super model. I know you know, come on darling; tell me whose car it is. I'm waiting.

Susan
I don't know who it belongs to. Could be Barry's new boyfriends, maybe he found himself a sugar daddy.

Nina
If that's so, then this new daddy must be a chubby chaser. Come on it's parked in front of your house. We're friends. Now who does the car belong to, hmm?

Susan
Nina, you're snooping around like a dog in heat. I don't know who it belongs to. What do I look like the FBI? *(Nina stares Susan down with a look).* All right stop glaring at me, it creeps me out.

It belongs to Lillian's son, Francis.

Nina
See how easy it is just to go ahead and tell me. *(Beat)* You mean her son Francis Bovell, the soap star, who plays the role of Cameron Blythe on the day time drama

"As the Evening Falls"

Susan
That's right! Now we move onto the bonus round.

Nina
I'm a big fan of that show. I haven't missed a single episode, well maybe one or two. Only because I had to take Edsel to the vet. Poor thing was choking on popcorn. Say is it possible to meet him?

Susan
I don't think that would be possible.

Nina
I've met hundreds of stars... I'm just dying to meet him.

Susan
I bet you are.

Antoine
(Entering from the bathroom). What about a celebrity like me?

Nina
I was talking about real people.

Antoine
I'm real people.

Nina
You're make believe. You're a fairy.

Antoine
Those apples? Come to poison us?

Nina
Morning Antoine.

Antoine
Morning Nina.

Nina
Lucky you, Susan. Francis Bovell here, what's he like, is he sexy off screen, is he dating anyone, male or female? Tell me.

Susan
I can't say. I don't know him that well.

Nina
How well do you know him, you can tell me.

Susan
I dare not. Listen you know how stars like their privacy.

Nina
That I do. Well I'll just leave these apples here. I have plenty, I would be gladly to bring more.

Susan
(Curtly) great, thanks.

Nina
Perhaps, I'll be by later to meet you know who. *(At this point sounds of Audrey whimpering and slight moans as she descends from the stairs).* What's that?

Susan
What's what?

Nina
That moaning noise. *(Susan covering again, and quickly takes the apples from Nina)*

Susan
I better take these apples to the kitchen, see ya Nina. *(Audrey enters crawling).*

Audrey
(Not paying any attention to the others, Nina turns back to meet her)
Has anyone seen my curlers?

Antoine
(Under his breath) God it's still crawling.

Audrey
Morning Susan, Morning Antoine. *(Noticing Nina for the first time)*
Hello.

Nina
Well hello there, and who might you be?

Antoine
Audrey, would you follow me to the kitchen for coffee?

Susan
Look at the time, so much to do, busy, busy, busy, later Nina.

Antoine
She's right, a lot to do. Bye bye.

Nina
Are you Lillian's new roommate?

Audrey
No, I'm her sister.

Nina
Hmm, sister huh, I'm Nina Chadwell, I live next door. Do you live
here, here with Lillian?

Audrey
Oh heavens no, I live on Van Ness, near the harbor.

Nina
Interesting.

Antoine
(Distracting Audrey away from Nina) Coffee Audrey!

Nina
(Persistent with question) What happened to your foot?

Audrey
My foor? Well that's a story let me tell you...

Susan
(Covering) No!... She sprained it, didn't you Audrey?

Nina
Hmm, I sprained my foot a few years back, not a nice thing, I was
trying to get the scoop on Madonna, while I was stepping down from
a curb, in front of the Hollywood Bowl. How did yours happen?

Antoine
(Jumping in) she sprained hers by stepping up onto a curb, in front
of the Manns Chinese Theatre. It was a premiere for Evita.

Nina

What a coincidence. *(Dog's bark in distance)* That must be my Edsel. Probably barking at my next dorr neighbor's rabbit Bunkie, poor thing is a mess. Oh the sight of that rabbit, it would make your hair stand on end, all mutated. You know she bought it from one of those research testing labs. The ones who test products on animals. Like shaving cream, shampoos, and lighter fluid. Well the little fury freak lives in her backyard. I told louis, it was just easier to get a dog. I think she sniffed glue as a child. Oh it's your gardener, Eli. Well I better be going. Nice to have met you Audrey, hope to know more about you. Susan, I still want to meet you know who. Ciao! *(As she exits out)* Morning Eli.

Eli

(From outside, stern voice) Morning Nina.

Audrey

Who did she say was here?

Susan

Eli, our gardener.

Audrey

Here, now? I don't look decent!

Antoine

Now she notices.

Susan

It's not going to matter.

Audrey

The hell it isn't.

Antoine

I can't bare to watch this or anything else around here. I'll be in the kitchen making coffee.

(Susan gives him the apples to take to the kitchen, Lillian enter in her wheelchair)

Lillian

Morning susan.

Susan
Morning Lillian, how did you sleep?

Lillian
Not well at all, but who has time to sleep their life away, when I have company to spend time with.

Audrey
I couldn't sleep either. *(Proudly)* I met your next door neighbor, Nina.

Lillian
Everything comes in threes.

Susan
She brought over some apples.

Lillian
Just what I need, more fiber in my diet. Antoine up yet?

Susan
He's in the kitchen making coffee, and Eli is here too.

Lillian
Eli's here early, he usually gets here around 10:30.

Audrey
Well he's here now. *(Doorbell rings)* That must be him, I'll be upstairs.

Lillian
Audrey, since you met Nina, I think you should meet Eli, he's a very nice man.

Audrey
Not now Lil. I'm on my way upstairs. *(She start to crawl for the stairs, while Susan goes to answer the door, Antoine enters from the kitchen, as if to answer the door as well.)*

Antoine
Audrey get up off of the floor, we have company. *(He see's Eli)* Oh it's Eli, carry on.

Lillian
Good morning Eli, come in, and what brings you here so early?

(Eli enters, he is a gentle looking man with gray temples, 40's. He's dressed in Khaki colored pants, brown shoes and a white shirt with the sleeves rolled up. As he enters, he takes off his gloves and wipes his boots on the door mat)

Eli
Morning, I fugured I get a head start on that project, you wanted me to do, putting more petunias around the walkway.

Lillian
Wonderful, Eli did you ever get a chance to meet my sister Audrey? She's been wondering who is it, that's done all that gorgeous landscaping in the back.

Eli
Hi, *(Noticing she's crawling)* Ma'am, did you loose something?

Susan
(Quickly covering) She lost an earring!

Lillian
A contact!

Antoine
Both!

Audrey
I didn't loose anything, well, except for my cat the other day, see I injured my foot by jumping...

Susan
By jumping off a curb!

Lillian
In front of a car.

Susan
And to avoid being hit, she twisted her ankle.

Lillian
By jumping over the car, and back onto the curb.

Audrey
I couldn't have said it better myself.

27

Eli
My God, some stunt woman you are, when did this happen?

Susan
Last week.

Lillian
Sometime during...

Antoine
Gay Pride.

Audrey
Yeah.

Eli
(Loosing interest) Oh, I see. *(He turns as if to leave).*

Lillian
But it happened on your way to work didn't it dear?

Audrey
Yeah, what she said.

Eli
I bet it's hard to get around the house with your foot all bandaged up like that?

Audrey
No, no trouble at all.

Antoine
Who is she kidding.

Eli
Well, I better get started. Nice to have met you Audrey, hope your foot heals fast. *(He exits)*

Antoine/Audrey
Me too.

Antoine
(Audrey exits back to her room) I'll just be getting back to making that pot of coffee.

Susan
Sometimes, I become more and more like you.

Lillian
Am I that bad of an influence on you?

Susan
(She looks about the room for Audrey's presence) Yes covering anything, that might embarrass her. I love her to death, bless her heart. When my husband Maurice died, it was very difficult to cope. There were too many things happening at once; The house, the bills, my demanding schedule for the show. Audrey was there for me, I don't want her to be embarrassed in front of other people. To her, it wouldn't matter one way or the other, but in some part of her it does, she cant' hide it from me, I know her better, than she thinks. *(She has some discomfort)* Oh, la, la. Mon Dieu!

Susan
Want another pain pill?

Lillian
No. I'll be fine, sometimes those pills make me too relaxed. It's alittle hard to breathe from time to time. Do you think Audrey has caught on yet?

Susan
I don't know, I don't think it's fair for you to keep it from her. She has to know sometime. What about Fancis and Mason, do they know?

Lillian
You and antoine are the only ones who know. I can't tell Audrey, she's a scatter brain, with her house being fumigated and this business of her crawling around on the floor, she's certainly not together. Mason and Fancis, I don't know when I'll tell them. They seem off balance. I'll find out what it is. *(Beat)* I didn't even want the network to know, but they had to know, I was under contract and Berny our producer, he knew something was wrong. So I didn't want to breech my contract, Berny let me go. Besides, there are people out there ready to sell sews to the tabloids. That's why I keep it away from Nina. Not that it's going to matter much longer. You're right, I can't keep going on with this masquerade of having a fractured hip.

29

Susan
Lillian, I wish, this didn't have to happen. Maybe there's a chance to slow the cancer dow, put it back into remission.

Lillian
I wish that too, but I'm too far gone for anymore treatments, I'm through with chemo. Believe me I want to keep what hair I have left, I want to look good until the end. Dr. Van Lornborg, nice doctor, he finally let me have the news last week, I have six months or less.

Susan
(Teary eyed) I can't believe, I'm losing someone so very special as you.

Lillian
Now, now, no tears. That's a girl *(Proudly)* I cetainly want to live out my remaining days as pleasant as possible, I've decided to make it easy on myself and everyone else. I'm going on vacation, somewhere tropical. Maybe the Bahamas or Brazil, or perhaps Barcelona, where do we French go eh? It's a last minute decision, but it's what I want. You see Susan I'm not really going, if you look at it that way, I'm going on vacation, and where ever I land, there I'll be, on a white sandy beach sipping some outrageous tropical drink, like a Bahama Mama, while looking out into the sunset.

Susan
Absolutely and you'll be too busy enjoying the warm sun, and the clear blue ocean, no time to e-mail anyone.

Lillian
Absolutely too busy. (Pause) Well, when I'm there, I'll send out postcards. Telling everyone I'm having a wonderful time! *(They laugh, then there is a pause)* And while I'm here until I leave I want to be gracious to the ones I love. Yes indeed, retired and on the beach. *(Pause)* Wish I was still working, *(beat)* miss my show and what a show it was! "An Evening with Lil Bovell", I never thought I would become a talk show host, after acting in the theatre. But I did, and damn it, I was great! What will they do without me...*(She ponders in thought for a moment)*

Susan
Something the matter, you need to lie down?

Lillian
No dear, I'm just thinking.

Susan
of what, the show? The sandy beach?

Lillian
No just thinking, other thoughts.

Susan
Ah, I know that look. Let me guess, you're got something planned. I can see the wheels turning in that head of yours.

Lilliam

You know me too well youg lady, but maybe this time I'll fool your ass.

Susan
Well in anycase, Ms. Bovell, I have to mail off letters for you and change your bedding. And later get those postcards for you.

Lillian
(she kisses her on the cheek) Remember postcards with tropical scenery. Thank you Susan. Someday you'll make a man vey happy.

Susan
What day, I'd like to know, call me if you need anything. *(She exits)*

Lillian
It'll be day that will surprise you. *(Mason entes from upstairs, in sweatpants and a tank top t-shirt, he stretches for his morning run)* Mason, Morning dear, what on earth are you doing?

Mason
Morning Ma'Ma, I was getting ready to go out on my morning run.

Lillian
So early dear, you didn't sneak in this morning till around 1:30 or 2:00.

Mason
I know, I am a bit tired.

Lillian
If you plan on running this morning dear, I believe Antoine is
making coffee, that should get your juices going.

Mason
Coffee, that sounds good right now. *(Lillian has another discomfort
moment)* Ma'Ma are you all right? Can I get you anything? It's
strange the last time we came to visit you were sick then. I recall you
had diarrhea.

Lillian
(Changing subject quickly) Is your brother up yet?

Mason
No, and let him sleep in, the grump.

Lillian
Is he in one of his moods again?

Mason
Of course he's in one of his moods, when is he not in a mood. It's all
because he doesn't like the way I'm writing for his character on the
show. He's having difficulty learning the lines for next week's show,
and blames me for it.

Lillian
That's Francis.

Mason
That's for sure. I've been stressed and under the gun with the
scheduling. I think my writing might be off.

Lillian
(Antoine enters from the kitchen) Ah, Antoine sweetie.

Antoine
Lillian, I apologize, I thought coffee was going smoothly, I bought
fresh beans, put them in the grinder, clean out the pot, apparently
Susan has never cleaned the coffee pot, since the Trojan War. And it
seems we're out of coffee filters.

Lillian
I believe, Susan, put them in the higher cupboard, when she was putting away the groceries this week.

Antoine
Are you sure?

Lillian
No, remember I slipped in the kitchen, "The forbidden territory"

Antoine
(Catching on) Right. Morning Mason don't you look cute. Say thanks for that ride in the Lamborghini last night. Would you like some coffee?

Mason
Sure.

Antoine
Cream or sugar?

Mason
Cream.

Antoine
My kind of man.

(He exits to the kitchen with a gleam in his eye).

Mason
I'm ready to go running. No, I'm too tired, I think I'll pass today. I should go...I don't know.

Lillian
Tough decision, to run or not to run.

Mason
Silly huh?, I mean I could just go for a walk, that would be exercise enough. No, I have become too obsessed with the idea of keeping in shape.

Lillian
There's nothing wrong with that, as long as you don't over do it.

Mason
True, I feel I needed to stay in shape, when Phillip, told me that I should, I was walking on egg shells, when I was with him.

Lillian
I heard the past tense of "was" Are you two still together?

Mason
Correct. Past tense as in, we're no longer together!

Lillian
Why? Was it because, you weren't keeping up with your daily morning runs?

Mason
No.

Lillian
Do you suppose the break up with Phillip has effected your writing?

Mason
I don't know. He's not who I thought he was.

Lillian
He's so different on the show, he seems so nice, very handsome.

Mason
That's his character, that's his acting. It's different when you live with them...Actors!

Lillian
He can't be that bad.

Mason
he is, I work around it all day, I got him that job working with Francis. He plays his brother Brandon on the show. Well, he would come home, I'd be busy writing for the next week's show, while he was getting ready to go out with his entourage, where he would secretly meet Stewart, another writer on the show, who's now an ex-friend of mine.

Lillian
So you knew this.

Mason
Of course I knew this, we were all working together.

Lillian
So is he still on the show?

Mason
(Beat) Yes as a matter of fact he is, a little favor of mine. I've written him a part, that he has been wanting to play for a very long time. Next week's episode, he stars as a Narcholeptic Priest, who's giving the final rights to Bubba, a prisoner, who is about to get the chair. And Bubba has been on death row for years and hasn't had Human contact...Physically. Phillip, Father Conner, is the character he portrays, has a Narcoleptic black out and falls to the ground with his mouth open when he awakes his pants are unbuttoned...*(Smiling)* It's really no stretch for Phillip to play.

Lillian
Really?

Antoine
(Entering) Lillian I'm sorry, but I looked up in the cupboard and I don't see the coffee filters.

Lillian
Try the second shelf in the pantry dear. *(He exits back to the kitchen with a childish pout)* Well what about all those other gorgeous guys on the show?

Mason
What about them?

Lillian
What about that nice looking actor Devon Pike, who plays Rick Hampton?

Mason
He doesn't even know, what the word commitment means, let alone how to spell it.

Lillian
OK, is there someone on that show that you like?

Mason
I'm through with actors!

Lillian
Some cute guy will come along. *(Antoine enters once again)*

Antoine
I'm sorry Lillian, but there are none in the pantry either.

Lillian
Antoine, soon I won't need that coffee, I could have gone to Columbia by now and brought back Juan Valdez.

Antoine
Then get him to make it! *(He exits to the bathroom)*

Mason
Should I help?

Lillian
it's all right, it's not cancer research. *(She has more discomfort)* Oh, ouch, oh my!

Mason
Are you OK?

Lillian
(Pretending) It's the hip, every time I turn.

Mason
Maybe you should take some time to relax.

Lillian
I'm fine honey. *(Antoine enters from the bathroom with a roll of toilet paper, making his way back to the kitchem)* Antoine, what are you going to do with that?

Antoine
I'm going to use it as a filter.

Lillian
I don't think so, I don't want my coffee tasting like April spring showers.

Mason
They bring out the May flowers. *(Starts out on his daily morning run)*

Lillian
Mason where are you going?

Mason
Now I feel like running, I'll get coffee later. *(He exits)*

Lillian
(Calling after him)
I thought this was going to be a visit. Ha!... Be careful!

Antoine
Well, what do I do now?

(Lillian gives a stare at him)

Lillian
Has it ever occurred to you to go to the store?

Antoine
Good idea, it just occurred. *(He exits out the front door)*

(Moments pass Lillian wheels herself over to the TV to play her video game, the sounds of the game bring Audrey downstairs)

Audrey
Lil, what are you doing?

Lillian
Audrey dear, you're up.

Audrey
I tried to get some sleep, but I thought I heard voices and weird noises. Oh it's the game you're playing.

Lillian
it's called Valkyrie's Revenge.

Audrey
Huh?

Lillian
To win you have to pick up these floating treasures to boost your
starship power; A pink triangle, a pair of Josephine's red pumps,
and Rubben's compact mirror. Then to get to the next level, you
have to capture the rainbow flag from your enemy, Queen Dookie.
Miss me Sucker!

Audrey
That sounds hard to play, a lot to remember.

Lillian
It's not that hard, I like to play, it makes the time go faster...*(To the
game)* No you don't, oh that was close, see I'm almost to the end of
this level, I need that powere boost...Ah...No! Shoot, I have one more
life left.

Audrey
Oh look out for that thing!

Lillian
That thing will destroy my starship.

Audrey
What are those green cookie shape things?

Lillian
Those are cookies, only they eat you.

Audrey
Oh.

Lillian
(To the game again) Son of a gun. You stupid thing! Ah missed that
floating space cube to boost my energy. I'm losing power...here they
come, here come the cookies. There I go.

Audrey
What happened? Did you loose because I was talking to you?

Lillian
No, I just can't get passed that level, too many giant cookies. Want
to play? Come on I'll teach you. Antoine showed me how to play,
and I'm almost as good as he is, I think I'm better.

Audrey
No lil, I don't think so, some other time.

Lillian
Come on it's fun just these two buttons to press, it's easy.

Audrey
I'm sure it is, but I can't imagine a grown woman like me playing a video game.

Lillian
Audrey don't be silly, I'm a grown woman playing a video game, what's the harm in that?

Audrey
(She glances over at the table where the vase once stood, that she broke) I might break some thing, like one of the buttons on the game.

Lillian
Audrey, just because you were startled last night and broke a vase doesn't mean you'll break everything. Hey we'll play another time.
Ok?

Audrey
OK. *(She start to exit back up stairs)*

Lillian
Audrey...

Audrey
Yes Lil. *(Beat)* What were you going to say?

Lillian
Don't stop having fun in you life.

Audrey
I do have fun.

Lillian
I know you better than that.

Audrey
How do you know?

Lillian
It doesn't seem like your enjoying life anymore.

Audrey
What a thing to say. You're only assuming that I'm not enjoying my life.

Lillian
I see you sometimes mope around the house. You stay in a lot, and how's this? When I call you at home, you're always there.

Audrey
So? You would be too if you hurt your foot, and it isn't as is I can go home. You've never had pests exterminated.

Lillian
Well who said you had to take in a roommate who brought roaches into your home. The termite story is good, I believed it, but don't worry I won't let your secret out. And your foot is only a minor sprain over your cat Cheeto who roams the streets and every alleyway looking for some muffin. Poor thing can't get laid, how can he, orange and puffy looking. And besides look at me, you're not in a wheelchair!

Audrey
(Imitating a line from Bette Davis) But ch'ya are Blanche, but ch'ya are.

Lillian
Audrey, we shouldn't bicker with one another. Life's too short.

Audrey
(Pause). You want to know something. *(Pause)*. I'm not young anymore.

Lillian
Of course you're not, that's a lame excuse. You think I'm young? Do you know what keeps me feeling young? It's my mind and my heart, sure the wrinkles of life are present on my face, but I also have age lines of laughter. For me I feel 20 again, how old are?

Audrey
Forty-five coming this September.

Lillian

Forty-five. Is that all? Yeah you're old. We better get the gun, it's too late to send you out to pasture. I'm 60 years alive and I love it! Age is in the mind, love is in my heart and playfulness is in my spirit. So what is age? A state of mind, age is for wine.

Audrey

I can't think like you do.

Lillian

You don't have to think like I do, think on your own. You used to be so wild and carefree and alive. Nothing ever seemed to get you down, not even a sprained foot. I remember when you broke your leg. The day you got the cast off, you went out dancing that night, remember?

Audrey

That's when Heubert was around.

Lillian

That cheating asshole!

Audrey

I still think about him. He might have cheated on me more than once while we were married, but there were some good times that we had together.

Lillian

Audrey, let it go. Get on with your life. Besides there are other men out there.

Audrey

Where am I going to find a man?

Lillian

I don't know. How long has it been since your divorce?

Audrey

It'll be five years in October.

Lillian

(Realizing) Wake up and smell yourself.

Audrey
I bathed this morning...I know, but where am I going to meet another man? I don't like going out. I don't have that many friends. It's certainly not safe for a woman to go out by herself nowadays. So tell me, who would take me out?

(The door bell rings).

Lillian
Maybe that's Antoine returning from the store, could you let him in please.

(Audrey goes to answer the door, she can't reach high enough to the peephole in the door, due to her injured foot, so she let's her crutches fall to the floor. She sees Eli).

Lillian
Who is it?

Audrey
It's the gardener man, what's his name?

Lillian
Eli.

Audrey
I guess. I'm out of here. *(She makes her way back up the stairs).*

Lillian
Audrey, where are you going? Are you going to answer the door? Some help you are. I'll get the door then, take your time dear. And if you fall you don't have far to go!

Audrey
Ha!

Lillian
Hello there Eli.

Eli
I don't mean to bother you again, I forgot to charge my cell phone battery. I tell ya you have to charge these babies all night long. When they were passing out charge, I thought they said Marge, I told them heck, I don't know her. *(He chuckles at his own bad joke).*

Lillian
Yeah, ok come in Eli.

Eli
I need to call the nursery, I hope they still have more of those miniature roses, I thought they would look nice in that smaller flower bed, near the fence. *(Noticing Audrey crawling on the floor again)* Hi, did you loose another contact, or an earring?

Audrey
No, I...

Lillian
She's stretching out her knees. Crutches can really take atoll on the ol' patellas.

Audrey
Not exactly.

Eli
Need some help up the stairs?

Audrey
I'm fine, I can manage.

Eli
I'd be glad to give you a hand.

Audrey
(A little bothered) I'm fine thank you. *(Lillian purposely runs over her hand with her wheelchair)* Ahhh! Lillian watch where you're wheeling that thing, you ran over my hand!

Lillian
(Playing match maker) Moi? Eli, could you be so kind and help Audrey off the floor.

Eli
Sure. Here allow me *(He accidentally steps on Audrey's same injured hand)*

Audrey
Ahhh! You're stepping on the same injured hand!

Eli

oops. I'm so sorry, clumsy me, are you all right? I can't believe I stepped on your hand, if you want to, you can step on mine.

Audrey
If I was able to, I would.

Lillian
Eli, let's just get her to the sofa, before someone else steps on her hand.

Eli
(Helping her to the sofa, he holds her hand, Audrey notices with a look) There you are, sorry about stepping on your hand, just stupid of me. Well, when they were passing out legs, I thought they said eggs, so I told them, I'll take a dozen. *(He chuckles)*

Audrey
O.K. That's all right, I'm fine now.

Eli
I bet you'll never look at street curbs the same way again. *(He goes to the phone)*

Susan
(Rushing in) What's going on, I heard someone screaming?

Lillian
Audrey.

Susan
Oh no, not again. Anymore broken vases?

Lillian
We've got it under control. Eli here helped her to the sofa.

Susan
Well, if you need me, just scream. *(She exits back into Lillian's room)*

Audrey
I want to say what wonderful job you're doing in the garden, everything is in full bloom, Agapanthas are so pretty and I love the smell of Jasmine in the air.

Eli

Thank you, I do my best. I'm going to plant those petunias around the walkway. Hope I have time. I was listening to the news and they mentioned the weather, something about Hurricane Davina up the coast of Mexico. It might hit here in San Francisco. Newscasters said perhaps thunder showers. If it does rain I don't think it'll be enough to damage the plants. . . Audrey are you all right, should I get something for your hand? An ice pack?

Audrey

I'm fine, it throbs a little but I can manage. I wish I had a wonderful garden like Lillian's, maybe when my house is rid of termites.

Eli

Termites, huh. How long have you had them?

Audrey

Oh I'd say I noticed them last year, when I had a roommate move in.

Eli

Really, last year? If that's so, they might have done a lot of damage. They can be destructive, nasty little buggers, chopping away at everything.

Audrey

Do they ever come back, once you get rid of them?

Eli

Well it depends on how you exterminate termites, there's a lot of ways these days. Now roaches... to get rid of them, sometimes it's a month to month process. Roaches can survive a nuclear disaster. A few days later they're back on the surface.

Audrey

I didn't know that.

Eli

They can be all over in your house, in your cabinets, across your sink, and counter tops, in your food, in your bed at night when you sleep, crawling all over...

Audrey
Please... I'm getting a visual.

Eli
Well better not dottle around here I have work to do. Sorry about stepping on your hand. It's been nice talking to you.

Audrey
Nice talking to you too.

Eli
Hope to see you around. *(He exits out the French doors)*

Audrey
Same here.

Lillian
He's a nice man.

Audrey
Wonderful green thumb he has.

Lillian
He makes it very pleasant around here. All the wonderful flowers are so pretty to look at. I love spending time out there. Maybe I could mention to him about working around your house.

Audrey
Oh Lil, I don't have enough yard to transform into paradise.

Lillian
Well, I'll still mention it to him, and don't worry about price, he's reasonable.

Audrey
Well maybe, I think I'll go lie down for awhile. *(She starts to get up from the sofa and has slight pain in the process)*. Ouch! Oh! Oh! *(She crawls away to her room. Susan enters with envelopes that look like they are ready to be mailed, she sees Audrey crawling, and gives her a look)*.

Susan
Audrey, should I get your crutches?

Audrey
No, I can manage *(As she continues to crawl away)*.

Susan
I'd be glad to get them for you.

Audrey
It's quite all right, sweetie, I can do this, piece of cake.

Susan
Ok if you say so. *(Audrey crawls off)*. I have everything just about finished with the letters, and the bills.

Antoine
(Entering from the front door, carrying a grocery bag). There you are... *(Demanding)*. Where are the coffee filters?

Susan
Pardon me?

Antoine
This morning, for your information, I was about to make a pot of coffee, but as I went into the kitchen simply to prepare a nice steaming cup of rich java, there wasn't a filter in sight to accomplish this little feat of mine. Oh yes, I looked everywhere and none to be found! *(As Susan is about to speak, Antoine cuts her off)*. We have plenty now until the next millennium, oh and I also bought some bagels and cream cheese.

Susan
Antoine, I can't believe you're so grumpy over coffee filter, there has to be more to it, what's going on?

Antoine
Get off my dress!

Susan
It's Victor. What has he done now?

Antoine
Victor and I have finally parted ways.

Susan
No, you haven't.

Antoine
Oh yes, we have.

Susan
Well there's always the internet... *(Antoine glares at Susan)*... Sorry

Antoine
Don't be. Victor sure isn't.

Lillian
What happened?

Antoine
It's an old cliché, he found someone else!

Lillian
Sorry, kiddo.

Antoine
It doesn't matter. He wore too much make-up..for me. I'd better put
this in the kitchen, and if there are no more obstacles, I'll get back
to making that pot of coffee. *(He enters the kitchen with the grocery
bag)*.

Susan
I better finish getting this mail out. How are you feeling? Can I get
you anything?

Lillian
No, I'm going to my room, I think I'm ready to take one of those
pain pills now.

Susan
Here let me help you to your room. *(She pushes the wheelchair)*.

Lillian
Thank you Susan.

*(Susan goes to the desk and talkes out from the drawer, the check book
and a few bills that she is finishing to mail off. A moment passes and
the voice of Francis is heard. He is rehearsing his lines for the show
"As the Evening Falls". He enters and doesn't even notice Susan in
the room)*.

48

Francis
And furthermore Brandon as my brother, you have to stop seeing Ellen. She's dangerous! She drove over little Timmy's hamster, "Squirts" with the mini van...

(He turns to continue, and Susan is staring at him from the desk). Oh hello Susan, I was so wrapped up in rehearsing these lines for the show, I didn't realize you were in here.

Susan
It's ok, I was just sealing these envelopes to be mailed off. If you need this room I can get out of your way.

Francis
You're fine, stay right there, I can study outside. *(He starts again with the script as he walks toward the French doors, to go outside).* Brandon, it would take a miracle to bring back poor little Squirts to life. And Brandon, the next thing you know it'll be you under the mini van...Ah these lines, what am I going to do?

Susan
Something the matter?

Francis
I'm having trouble with remembering the lines. I think it's the script, probably Mason's writing, I don't know.

Susan
Maybe if you had someone to rehearse with, would that help?

Francis
It just might, I could use all the help I can get. Wait you're busy with things, you probably got a lot to do.

Susan
I'm almost done.

Francis
Are you sure, I'm not keeping you from anything?

Susan
No, not at all, I would love to rehearse with you.

Francis
On that note how could I resist.

Susan
Where would you like me to start.

Francis
Ok. On this page, read the lines opposite mine.

Susan
Mildred Princeton?

Francis
Right.

Susan
Cool, I like this. Where do I read?

Francis
Let's see...*(He turns a page in the script)* Right here on page 22,
starting with Mildred's line, "Cameron, it's so hard to see you here".

Susan
I must tell you I haven't acted since high school drama, my reading
might be a little off.

Francis
No problem, you'll do fine.

Susan
(Reading as Mildred Princeton, in a cold reading fashion) "Cameron
it's so hard seeing you here".

Francis
That's good. *(He reads the part of Cameron Blythe)* Mildred, why
did you come here?

*(Susan starts to get into the reading of the script, she takes every
chance to look at Francis, as he paces for a moment then they are face
to face).*

Susan
I couldn't stay away. It's so hard not seeing you around.

50

Francis
Thank you Mildred, for your concern I'll be all right.

Susan
And leave you here? What have they done to you? This place is awful.

Francis
It's not, stop worrying.

Susan
You're lying to me, you know it's awful. You're just saying that so I don't worry about you.

Francis
Mildred, please go, I don't want you to see me like this.

Susan
What will I do in the meantime, huh tell met that?

Francis
You'll just have to wait it out.

Susan
But how long, Cameron, how long should I wait?

Francis
It's almost over, then we'll be in each other's arms soon.

Susan
Cameron my love, when?

Francis
Please, Mildred, you're nagging again.

Susan
It's going to be very hard waiting for you, Cameron.

Francis
I know you will get along fine without me. *(He then goes out of character)*. This is where the nurse enters, I think we need a third person to read.

Susan
No problem, I can read both parts. *(She reads Nasaly as the nurse).*
Ma'am, visiting hours are over. *(Then reading as Mildred)* Please,
just a little longer. Please. *(As the nurse)* I'm afraid not, miss.
Doctor's orders. They're getting Mr. Blythe ready for surgery. *(As Mildred)* No!!

Francis
Please, Mildred, do as the nurse says. It's best for you to go.

Susan
(As Mildred). I'll stay until you recover.

Francis
(Going out of character again). Hmmmm. Oh, that's a misprint. She
says "Until you're out of surgery".

Susan
Oh. I'll stay until you're out of surgery.

Francis
What will I do without you, Mildred?

Susan
(As the nurse) Miss, you'll have to wait in the waiting room. Come,
I'll show you the way. *(As Mildred).* I believe I know the way.
Thank you.

Francis
This is where the doctor enters the room.

Susan
(As the Doctor). How are we doing, My. Blythe?

Francis
Fine, Doctor.

Susan
(As the Doctor). Is there any discomfort?

Francis
A little, Doctor.

Susan

(As the Doctor). Don't you worry, Mr. Blythe. We'll take care of that in surgery.

Francis

Will I be able to... You know...?

Susan

Sure Mr. Blythe, surgery on your prostate is not that difficult. *(Susan bursts out laughing and goes out of character).* Sorry I didn't mean to laugh. You're in the hospital for prostate surgery?

Francis

Uh huh, and probably next week's show I'll have erectile dysfunction.

Susan

Are you back in surgery?

Francis

Who knows, with Mason's writing, his imagination scares me.

Susan

Would you like to read more?

Francis

Sure, there is a better scene before the hospital. *(He flips through the pages in the script. A crash is heard in the kitchen).*

Antoine

(From inside the kitchen). Ouch! Son of a. . . Damn Tupperware!

Susan

That sound like Antoine in the kitchen, I better see what happened. *(She enters the kitchen).*

Francis

If he's cooking noodles, don't go in there!

Susan

(Exiting from the kitchen). I think he's planning a Tupperware party. Now where were we?

Francis

On page 36, right here, is where Mildred comes in.

Susan
(Holding the script again, there is a slight pause). It starts with your line.

Francis
Right. Don't tell me...Let me think...What's the first word of the line?

Susan
Here.

Francis
Here...

Susan
Uh huh.

Francis
Here...here what?

Susan
Here we...

Francis
OK, don't tell me. Here we are?

Susan
Nope. Here we go.

Francis
Here we go? . . I know this... here we go again?

Susan
No here we go, that.

Francis
Here we go that?

Susan
Uh huh.

Francis
That, that...What's the whole line? I can't get it.

Susan
Here we go, that ought to be enough wood.

Francis
Right. Now I've got I.

Susan
From the top?

Francis
Yeah. "Here we go, that to be enough wood".

Susan
(As Mildred). It's cold in here.

Francis
(As Cameron). It will warm up in a moment. Do you want my jacket?

Susan
No, I want your arms around me. Keep me warm.

Francis
(He proceeds to put his arms around Susan from behind her). We haven't done this in awhile.

Susan
We haven't been to your cabin in awhile.

Francis
Look, the fire is going.

Susan
Sure is.

Francis
It should heat up the room in a few moments.

Susan
(Sexy). Or something else will.

Francis
Hmmm.

Susan
Hold me. Hold me tight and don't let go..Your arms feel nice around me.

Francis
you feel nice to hold. *(Going out of character)*. I'm sorry. This isn't the scene either.

Susan
But you were doing so nicely on the lines. You didn't miss a word.

Francis
Really?

Susan
Really. . . And what's wrong with that scene?

Francis
I don't know. I feel off today.

Susan
With the lines?

Francis
Uh huh... I don't know.

Susan
Do you want to try again?

Francis
The lines?

Susan
Yeah.

Francis
Sure.

Susan
(Both go back into character). It's nice to be held.

Francis
Why did you want to come..?

Susan
To be with you.

Francis
As we are now?

Susan
Exactly as we are now.

Francis
It's warming up in here now.

Susan
It certainly is.

Francis
I missed you.

Susan
I missed you, too. Don't let go. Keep your arms around me. I'd
rather be warmed by you then by the fire.

Francis
Yeah?

Susan
Yeah. I couldn't ask for more.

Francis
You might.

Susan
I might.

Francis
You're trembling.

Susan
It's because you make me feel so safe, and I feel secure in your arms.

Francis
You do?

Susan
Yes. You're the man I want to be with.

Francis
And you're the woman I want to be with.

Susan
Don't let go. Hold me closer to you.

Francis
How's this? Close enough?

Susan
Oh, Cameron.

Francis
Yes?

Susan
Kiss me, Cameron.

Francis
Mildred, I love you.

Susan
Kiss me Cameron. . . kiss me. . . kiss me. *(She gets carried away and kisses Francis).* They kiss each other. *(Lillian enters, sees them, but doesn't speak, she stays a distance from them. Susan pulls away).* I didn't meant to. . . I guess I got carried away.

Francis
Whoa, I didn't mind. I mean it was great.

Susan
The kiss? No I didn't mean the kiss.

Francis
Please. The kiss was part of the acting.

Susan
How could I get carried away like that? How foolish.

Francis
It's OK. Believe me I never had a rehearsing partner that could do that. . . *(Lillian meaning not to make noise she does by bumping the desk chair).* Ma'ma.

Susan
Lillian?

*(At this moment Francis has developed an erection, caused by Susan.
He quickly on the sofa, covering his problem with a pillow).*

Lillian
I couldn't rest. Oh, Francis, you're finally up. I don't' want to
bother you two. I just came in to get some coffee. Although that has
been a difficult commodity to get around here.

Susan
Maybe some tea?

Lillian
That sounds good. Oh I must be in the way, I noticed you were
rehearsing lines.

Francis
I was glad Susan offered to help.

Lillian
And what a partner to rehearse with.

Susan
(Embarrassed). Oh stop.

Lillian
You're becoming quite the little actress. Nicely done dear, I better
get out of your way and let you two get back to that scene.

Susan
*(She picks up the bills and other letters from the desk, but puts them
back down).* I'll get your tea Lillian, stay right there.

Lillian
That's all right, Antoine is bringing me coffee. Which seems to be a
tough commodity around here.

Susan
Then I'll mail these letters off. *(She picks up the letters, passes by
Francis on her way out, quickly handing him back his script, the she
exits out).*

Francis
(He raises with the script covering his embarrassed erection). I'll just be in here Ma'ma.

(He exits upstairs).

(Antoine exits from the kitchen with Lillian's coffee).

Antoine
Well the coffee is finally made. Here you go. Sorry it took so long, I had to clean up after Susan, what a mess she made. Oh my head. . . Damn Tupperware. If you need me, just ring the bell.

(He exits upstairs).

Lillian
(Door bell rings). Speaking of bells, *(She wheels herself to answer the door, Nina stands before her with a chocolate cake).* Nina, what brings you here?

Nina
Oh nothing really, *(She looks about the room).* Well I won't stay long, I brought you a double mint chocolate cake. I baked it last night.

Lillian
How sweet of you. *(She hesitates to take it from Nina).*

Nina
Go on, it's safe to eat, I haven't tainted the chocolate frosting with anything.

By the way how's the hip?

Lillian
Fine, just fine, a little uncomfortable at times but I manage.

Nina
I understand you have company?

Lillian
Company?

Nina
Yes company. There is a Lamborghini parked in front of your house.

Lillian
Lamborghini? *(Quickly).* It's Barry's from next door, he got a raise at work.

Nina
I've hear that line before.

Lillian
I mean, his sister gave him the money.

Nina
He doesn't have a sister.

Lillian
That's because, Bobby had a sex change, his job paid for it.

Nina
If you're going to lie, do it right.

Lillian
Yes. *(Beat)* my two sons are here visiting.

Nina
That's wonderful, especially Francis, your son from the soap "As the Evening Falls" say is it possible to meet him?

Lillian
Well he's very private.

Nina
How private is he? Tell me. *(Eli enters from outside the door that Nina left open).*

Eli
Hello anyone home?

Lillian
Eli come in, come in.

Eli
Hello Lillian. . .*(Stern).* Hello Nina.

Nina
Hello.

Lillian
Let me guess, you didn't get the miniature Roses. The nursery was
out of them?

Eli
No, I got the roses, and I was about to plant them in the back, when
I came across these huge holes, tons of dog droppings and flowers
scattered everywhere. It looked like a war zone.

Lillian
In my backyard?

Eli
Yes there's turds everywhere, you can't walk around out there
without stepping on one.

Nina
That must be some big dog.

Eli
I thought Godzilla was loose in the neighborhood.

Lillian
I wonder whose dog it could be.

Eli
Where is your dog Nina?

Nina
Why Eli, you don't suspect my Edsel would do such a thing.

Eli
Just asking, where is your dog?

Nina
Nonsense, he's in my backyard.

Eli
Really, I saw him earlier in Lillian's garden.

Nina

That's a lie, my Edsel can't get loose from my yard. And if he could, why would he dig up Lillian's flowers and do his business everywhere?

Eli

I don't know you tell me.

Nina

My dog is not some poopie bandit, he didn't do it.

Eli

I know he did and you probably coaxed him with a milk bone to do it, so you can get a story on Lillian's two sons.

Nina

Get real.

Lillian

(Trying to clear the matter so she doesn't want a write up in Nina's paper). Now Eli. Maybe it was someone else's dog that got into the garden.

Nina

That's what happened, some other dog did it.

Eli

I don't think so, we should compare the droppings.

Lillian

Eli, I wouldn't advise it.

Nina

What are you crazy?

Lillian

Please, you two, it's not big of a deal.

Eli

They're big all right at least a foot long. I know your dog did it.

Nina

How can you prove it?

Eli
We'll measure them! *(As he pulls out a tape measure)*.

Nina
You sick freak!

Eli
Come here I'll show you. *(Eli exits through the French doors, leaving them open to the garden outside. Nina Dumbfounded, but determined to be vindicated follows. Mason enters)*.

Mason
What is going on down here, some kind of riot?

Lillian
No, the turd world war.

Mason
(As he looks out the doors). With your next door neighbor?

Lillian
Uh huh, it'll be on Real TV tonight.

Nina
I'm telling you it's not my dog!

Eli
Face it you know it to be true! Don't lie to me or anyone in this backyard! *(Susan enters from the front door)*.

Nina
This is foul play on your part, I know it!

Eli
Listen you, I don't like you, in fact I hate you!!

Susan
Whose in the back yelling, is it Audrey again?

Lillian
No dear I'm about to be ruined.

Nina
That doesn't measure 12 inches! *(Francis enters from upstairs)*.

Francis
Who's screaming outside? I'm trying to study my lines here. Who's out there?

Mason
You wouldn't believe it.

Eli
Don't you dare pick that up it's evidence! *(Antoine enters).*

Antoine
What's going on, why all the noise? What is everyone looking at? Is that Nina and Eli outside yelling at one another? Maybe they'll physically hurt each other. This I gotta see. *(He moves in with the others).*

(The sound of thunder).

Susan
Wow thunder, that storm moved in quickly.

Lillian
Hey you two Stop it! There's a storm coming. *(Thunder again, Which brings Audrey downstairs).*

Audrey
Lillian, Lillian!

Lillian
In here Audrey!

Nina
You're still pissed off about that article, that's what this is all about, isn't it?

Eli
Maybe.

Nina
Oh shut up!

Eli
No, you shut up!

Audrey
Who's outside?

Antoine
The turd warriors.

Audrey
(Thunder sounds again). Ooh thunder.

Susan
It's Hurricane Davina, it came up from down south. *(Thunder again)*.

Lillian
That was loud, please you two come inside let's settle this as adults!

Eli
You are so sleazy, I still think, it was your dog that did it.

Nina
You deceitful little man!! You garden weasel!

Eli
Deceitful huh? You're a big liar, with your rumors about people!
Look at all this dog do...Liar!

(Lightening flashes)

Mason
Whoa, did you see that lightening?

Francis
That came close. *(Lightening flash again)*.

Lillian
Come inside you two before you both get struck by lightening!
(Thunder sounds again the a flash of light, then the house lights flicker. Suddenly Nina and Eli retreat inside the house, then there is another flicker of the lights and then black out).

Audrey
There go the lights.

Nina
Damn rolling blackouts!

Eli
Who's holding my hand?

Audrey
Who's holding mine?

Susan
Excuse me, who's that? . . Oh!

Antoine
Hey! Who's touching me?

Mason
Antoine?

Nina
(Dog's bark) Edsel my baby!

(There is sound of rain falling and the lights come up quickly, all are frozen in place. Lillian is faced up next to a wall in the house feeling her way around. Nina on the steps of the French doors. Francis and Susan are locked into a passionate kiss. Eli and Audrey embraced in each other's arms. While Mason holds Antoine off of the floor in his arms, Antoine's head is leaning on Mason's shoulder).

Antoine
(An aside to the audience, as a southern bell) A man, man, what it is to be in a man's arms again.

(Lights out quickly)

End of act I Scene 2

ACT II

(At rise, 4 hours later, the house is disorganized from the chaotic thunder storm. Susan & Antoine clean the living room. Antoine is vacuuming the floor, Susan is picking up sofa pillows, etc, etc. The door bell rings Susan looks at Antoine to answer the door, but he turns his head to ignore the door, Suan gives in and goes to the door, signaling Antoine to turn off the vacuum cleaner).

Susan
(Answering the door). Nina.

Nina
(Storming in). Where is Lillian?

Susan
She wasn't feeling too well, she's lying down in her room. I wouldn't
disturb her.

Nina
This is it! *(Drops a black plastic trash bag on the livingroom floor).*

Antoine
What's that?

Nina
Take a look.

Antoine
No way, It's probably some paper boy who didn't deliver your paper.
(Nina opens the bag, shows them the contents).

Susan
Don't . . .

Antoine
Oh. . .

Susan
Shit!

Nina
And it was left on my door step by Eli, The Terrible.

Susan
Why would Eli do such a thing?

Nina
It's not my Edsels, I compared!

Antoine
Compared?

Nina

I know they're not his, his are smaller, these are too large! It's your! *(She starts to leave).*

Antoine

Hey, missy, *(More flamboyant)* come back here and get this shit off the carpet!

Nina

It's not mine!

Antoine

It's not ours either, we don't have a dog!

Susan

Pick this up Nina! We're cleaning.

Nina

So am I. This place needs a lot of cleaning.

Susan

Wait a damn minute!

Nina

(Stronger exit line).

Get the vacuum, get to it! You little cleaning Drones! *(She exits quickly).*

Antoine

(Yelling). I hope a house falls on you!

Susan

Who does she remind you of?

Antoine

Norman Bate's Mother!

Susan

What do we do with this?

Antoine

Be careful, this might get messy.

(Lillian enters the room).

69

Lillian
How's it coming?

Susan
Rough.

Antoine
Lillian, Nina was just by, and brought over a surprise.

Lillian
Oh how sweet of her and after all the business between her and Eli
in the garden.

Susan
Very sweet.

Antoine
So sweet you can smell it.

Lillian
I bet it's her brownies.

Susan
Same color.

Antoine
Here look.

Lillian
What is it? *(She opens the bag and looks in it)*. Oh shit!

Susan
Uh huh.

Antoine
She says it's yours.

Lillian
Mine? What the hell does she mean? Besides I haven't seen
anything that solid in months.

Antoine
Best thing for that is to eat more cheese.

Lillian
She's pissing me off!

Antoine
That's the spirit Lillian.

Lillian
Damn Her!

Susan
Antoine, don't encourage her.

Lillian
I ought to go over there and give it back.

Susan
Lillian, don't. She'll write about it and put it in that crummy tabloid of hers the next week . . . Remember your health.

Lillian
Yeah, yeah, come on you two, we're paying that gift giving shit of a broad a visit!

Antoine
Charge!

Lillian
Viva la France! *(As they exit).* She can't give me shit and get away with it!

(Audrey enters on her crutches and is walking to the kitchen, when the phone rings).

Audrey
(Answering the phone).

Hello. . . Yes this is the Bovell residence...No this isn't Mrs. Bovell, this is her sister...May I ask who's calling? Pardon?...The doctor's office... Hold on I'll get her for you. *(Audrey calls out for Lillian but there is no answer).* I'm sorry but she isn't here, she must have stepped out. If you like, to leave a message for her, I'd be glad to give it to her. *(Audrey picks up the bundle of postcards on the desk and examines them).* . . . Could you please repeat that?. . . Uh huh, spell the last name...Dr. Van Lornborg, from the oncology center,

Lillian has a scheduled appointment at 10:15am, Wednesday, June 11th . . . Sure will..*(A little confused by the phone call)*.. Thank you. *(She hangs the phone up and puts the cards backup and reads the back of one)*. Bon Voyage everyone, it will be a great get away, going on a vacation cruise, don't write back, I'll be to busy on the beach with my Cabana boy Ruddy and his two brothers, I can't say their names too many R's to roll. Love you all, dearest Lil. Who the hell is Ruddy, what's this vacation business, what about her hip?

(The door bell rings).

Eli
(Audrey answering the door). Hello there Audrey. Is Lillian around?

Audrey
No, I haven't seen her.

Eli
I just need to use the phone again, Sorry to bother you, but I dropped my cell phone in the backyard pond. Just hope those fish don't use up my 200 free minutes. *(He chuckles)*.

Audrey
Ah, yeah, come in. You can use that phone. The battery is charged on that one. *(She smiles)*.

Eli
(Dials phone).

Hello, is this Mr. Thomasini? Hey how the hell are ya? Good. Just busy as usual, uh huh, . . Well what I need is . . . your store still have those Morning Glories on sale? Good, and what time do you close today?. . .Great thanks, you too. *(Hangs up the receiver)*. Well I'm off to the nursery again. Tell Lillian I'll be back to plant those Morning Glories along the fence, that's if we can ever keep that dog out!

Audrey
Nina's dog?

Eli
Edsel, big thing, have you seen her dog? Ugly mutt, with an under bite, *(He shows Audrey his Edsel impression, he barks like the dog)*. Monster dug up the Morning Glories and attacked the Calla Lilies and dirt everywhere.

Audrey
Lillian is going to be upset.

Eli
I know, she'll be upset all right, that's why I paid Nina a visit with a bag of her own dog's droppings, and left it on her doorstep. Too bad it wasn't her birthday.

Audrey
Eli how could you?

Eli
Very easy, I just picked the bag up and walked to her doorstep and dropped it there. I wonder if she'll send me a card to thank me.

Audrey
That is going to be one angry lady.

Eli
Good. I know that it isn't any of my business to do such a thing, but there was a time when that bitch wrote about me and your sister. That Lillian and I were lovers. Later there was another article, about Lillian being abducted by aliens and turned into a vegetarian lesbian.

Audrey
That's a bunch of bull, I would know if my sister was a vegetarian.

Eli
Well, that year Lillian threatened to sue her, she told Nina to keep her business out of hers. I was having trouble, I couldn't get my wife to believe that it was just some filthy rumor, that Nina wrote about me and Lillian. The rumor was, I was always tending Lillian's garden whenever I could, planting my tulips on her rosebuds, while sowing my oats. That same year after, the so called article came out. My wife divorced me. So I haven't remarried.

Audrey
Sorry about your divorce, Nina, what a wicked lady.

Eli
She's beyond that, the devil asks her for suggestions.

73

Audrey

It's had to belive what rumors can do. They can destroy a lot if you let them. Well I guess we have something in common. I'm divorced, but mine was caused by, shall we say, another woman. Huebert, was seeing my therapist for a different kind of treatment.

Eli

Did you ever remarry?

Audrey

No I haven't found the right man, I don't want to step into that role of marriage again.

Eli

Me either *(Beat)* I better get back to work. *(He starts out).* Thanks for letting me use the phone.

Audrey

Eli, before you go, can I ask you something?

Eli

Sure.

Audrey

Knowing, that it's none of my business, but I feel I must know, do you know if Lillian is having Chemo Therapy?

Eli

I wouldn't know.

Audrey

I just got a phone call from a receptionist at the Oncology Center.

Eli

Hmm, I wouldn't make too much of it, perhaps the receptionist got the wrong number.

Audrey

Maybe, but she seemed very clear about who she was scheduling the appointment for.

Eli

I wish I could help, but I stay out of my clients business. Well in any case, I better get started.

Audrey
You're right. I need some fresh air. Mind if I walk out with you?
It's such a beautiful day.

Eli
Sure, here let me help you.

Audrey
Thank you. *(She leans her crutches against the wall next to the
French doors as if she could walk all along, they exit out together,
then we hear the voices of Lillian, Antoine and Susan from outside of
the house. A moment passes then they enter).*

Antoine
Go ahead see if we care, look do yourself a favor take more Prozac!

Susan
You wicked ol' witch! *(She lams the door).*

Lillian
The nerve of that woman! She shouldn't be allowed to breed!

Susan
She irks me!

Lillian
Do you think it's true, that Eli dropped it on her doorstep?

Antoine
If he did, you should give him a raise.

Lillian
(More discomfort). Oh, ca fait mal! Ouch! I could use some water, I
feel like crap. Ha crap!!

Susan
I'll get it for you. *(She goes to the kitchen, Antoine adjusts Lillian in
her chair).*

(Mason and Francis enter)

Remind me never to go with you again. We almost got mobbed by
your friggin' fans photographers everywhere. One of them thought
I was your agent and another asked how long we've been seeing each
other. Oh won't that make a lovely made for TV movie. We'll get

Aaron Spelling to do it!

Francis
Calm down. I told the guy at the auto shop to set my appointment
away from everyone else's.

Mason
Apparently there was a breakdown in communication. Two simple
things: get the car's oil changed and pick up blank discs for my lap
top and it turns out to be a scene from the Titanic!

Francis
Sorry next time I'll go alone!

Mason
Damn right you will...Antoine...Where is everyone? What happened
to the house. The Hurricane. Oh God where is Ma'ma, oh Francis
she's gone. I can't breathe. She was probably outside and got swept
up by the wind in her wheelchair.

Francis
You'll have to excuse my brother, he's never been the same since the
accident.

Antoine
(To Mason). We were cleaning, we're domestics *(He picks up more of
the pillows and arranges them on the sofa)*.

Mason
Francis...Ah, why do I listen to you!

Antoine
Rough time?

Mason
We had a hectic day.

Antoine
Better than having a shitty one.

Lillian
(Lillian enters with Susan pushing the wheelchair behind her). Ahh
my prodigal sons have returned.

Mason
We would have been back earlier, but Francis had to stop to sign autographs for all of San Francisco. It took forever, I thought we'd never get home. It seemed longer than the O.J. Trial.

Francis
Oh stop crying, I had to sign a few autographs for some people who saw me when I took the car into have the oil changed.

Mason
(To Francis). Never mind. Ma'ma feeling better?

Lillian
Fine a little tired.

Francis
Well soon your hip will be healed and you'll be up walking and back to your old self again.

Lillian
Huh?

Francis
Your hip.

Lillian
Hip .. right, my hip feeling better.

Susan
You should lie down and take it easy.

Lillian
I guess that visit with Nina took a lot out of me.

Antoine
I don't know about that, you're a tough ol' bird.

Lillian
And don't you forget it.

(Eli and Audrey enter from the garden laughing and cheery).

Audrey
Now that was fun. *(Eli helping her down from the step).* Thank you.

Eli
You're welcome.

Audrey
I haven't done that in a long time.

Antoine
What did she do, get lucky?

Susan
Audrey, you're walking.

Francis
Well, well, well look at you, up on your feet. Good for you.

Antoine
There is a God.

Lillian
You two were outside in the garden?

Audrey
Uh huh, it's lovely out there. Eli has done wonders with the landscaping, you should see all the flowers are blooming and humming birds everywhere, they're so pretty, so delicate.

Lillian
Wonderful, good to see you walking around kiddo. So you like my little garden of Eden?

We'll just have to have Eli do the same for your place.

Audrey
I don't know about my place, too many weeds, I haven't gone back there in along time, God knows what I'll find back there. Maybe some bones from a dinosaur. Everything looks fine except some big holes that Nina's dog dug up.

Lillian
I'm glad you brought that up Eli, were you the instigator of the little episode over at Ms. Chawells?

Eli
I must admit, it was me.

Antoine
So it was you.

Eli
She started that loony. I wanted to teach her a lesson! That dog
of hers dug up all the Morning Glories that I planted, and crap
everywhere. I could only take so much of it. That'll give her
something to write about!

Lillian
That's what I'm afraid of.

Eli
You can't let her walk all over you like that. It sure was great seeing
her pissed off it made my day.

Francis
That's all I need, bad press.

Lillian
Now, now. It'll be all right.

Francis
I heard that before. Next thing I know I'll be on the front page of
some paper, headline reading, Francis Bovell career sinking, going
to the dogs. Bow wow.

Lillian
Let's just let things cool down. If all goes right, she'll realize how
ridiculous all this is and expect an apology and that'll be it . . I hope.

Eli
Well she won't be over for awhile, that's a good sign. Listen I'll
make it up to you. I've got some wonderful landscape ideas waiting
for you. But in the meantime I've always wanted to meet you Mr.
Francis Bovell, could you sign my shovel for me?

Francis
I'd be glad to.

Eli
Thank you, could you sign it there, my "Dear old green thumb chum, Eli".

(Francis signs the shovel).

Eli
Thank you so kindly, I'll be seeing you around *(He exits to the garden).*

Francis
Now, that's different. Signing a shovel, what a kick. People will have anything autographed.

Mason
Yeah, that was the one he was using in the backyard to shovel the you know what.

Francis
(In disgust). Oooh. This is where I exit to the bathroom.

Mason
I've got work to do.

Audrey
What a beautiful day, I think I'll go for a walk.

Antoine
Listen to little Mary sunshine. Go for a walk, she's possessed.

Audrey
Anyone care to join me?

Susan
You shouldn't walk alone, I'll join you.

Lillian
Be careful out there.

Audrey
Don't worry sweety, I'm packing pepper spray.

Antoine
(To Susan). If you and the scarecrow are going to see the wizard, mind if I tag along?

Susan
Sure thing Dorothy. I'm sure those ruby slippers will take you where you need to go.

Audrey
Wait a minute, kids, I need to get my glasses and money for the BART, I thought we'd go across the bay.

Antoine
BART? Across the bay? . . . I know she's sick, I can feel it in my cheeks.

Susan
(Reassuring Lillian). We shouldn't be gone long. Will you be alright?

Lillian
If I need anything I have Francis and Mason here.

Susan
OK, we'll hurry back.

Lillian
No hurry, you need sometime away from me.

Susan
Are you sure?

Lillian
Go for that walk, get some fresh air, and stop and smell the flowers...
Besides I love seeing my sister full of energy.

Antoine
Energy, yeah she'll be outside roller blading. *(Audrey re-enters, in hat with a flower in it, and sunglasses).*

Audrey
Ok, lets hit it. *(They exit, while Antoine lags behind).*

Antoine
(Jokingly). Here we go trah, la, la. *(Francis exits from bathroom, then exits to kitchen).*

Lillian
Francis where are you going?

Francis
I thought I'd have a cup of coffee and rehearse my lines in the kitchen.

Lillian
Coffee, good luck on getting a cup, wait no more I love you's?

Francis
I'm sorry, what can I get you?

Lillian
Just a warm visit. Like you promised, sit down relax, life's too short.

Francis
I know I've done a lousy job of visiting, sorry. I shouldn't of came here with work on my mind, something is missing.

Lillian
What do you mean?

Francis
Like something is not there for me. I love the job. I have Mason to thank for that. If it hadn't been for him I would still be back at that crummy little radio station, working that boring night shift. I don't know what's wrong with me. I seem out of it.

Lillian
Well you seem a little off balance.

Francis
I think you're right, I do seem off balance.

Lillian
Francis if the lines are what's making you off balance, well you know as I know, that every actor, no matter how talented they are will have difficulty learning their lines. It goes with the job. I use to have trouble learning them all the time, remember when I was on that television show, that police drama, "Mick Reno" Where I played Jan Hatfield the coroner's wife who did all the autopsies. I didn't know anything about all that medical jargon, but I learned real quick. Then when the producer at Fox gave me a chance to have my own talk show, I grabbed it with both hands, Never had to learn a single line again, well almost. When we had the snake handler on the show. . .weirdo.

(She moves into Francis)

Lillian
Now Francis, I'm not asking you to become a talk show host, some of them are short lived. But it's like what we are doing now, sitting here chatting having a warm visit. I remember Merv Griffith asked me to be on his show, another host to be on his show, well I was nervous, I said to myself, I wonder what he wants me for? What am I going to say, what should I talk about and not talk about. Then I was asked on Mike Douglas's show, he was wonderful. What I'm saying is Francis, if your shoes are on too tight relax, loosen up and take a deep breath and relax, and if you do that, then the lines will come to you. Just visit with me for awhile, we may not get to do this again.

Francis
My shoes are not on too tight, I am relaxed. It's the damn lines. It's Mason's terrible writing!

Lillian
That's because his break up with Phillip, it had something to do with his writing he told me all about it.

Francis
He knows not to bring personal matters into work.

Lillian
I don't think it's all bad, especially when you were rehearsing with Susan.

Francis
Oh you figured that one out. She's a great reading partner, not to mention a fantastic kisser.

Lillian
See sparks are all ready flying.

Francis
Ya know, I never seen someone so committed to reading a character out of a script. That kiss made my day!

Lillian
Really?

Francis
Well she's attractive, and there's something about her, that. . .That makes me feel different when I'm around her.

Lillian
Uh huh.

Francis
I'm not turned on every time a girl kisses me. Debbie used to do that for me.

Lillian
Used to, aren't you two still together?

Francis
I don't want to go into that right now.

Lillian
Are you two having problems?

Francis
I don't care if she falls off the face of the earth!

Lillian
Well that answers it.

Francis
She's very deceiving, played me like a chess game, knew every move to make. She's very handy at using cards too, credit cards!

Lillian
Well, you do have money, sometimes those people are out there.

Francis
True, I'm glad I knew something was up with her, or she would have sucked every penny I had out of me, the leech!

Lillian
I think she's been on your mind and this is causing you to loose focus on you lines.

Francis
Very much so. It's over between us, she's gone. She's with some other guy. And your right she has been on my mind, causing me to loose concentration on learning these lines for the show.

Lillian
Well it seems that everyone is in the same boat with these bad relationships.

Francis
What do you mean?

Lillian
Mason, with Phillip, You with Debbie, Audrey divorced, Antoine's break up with Victor, Eli and his ex-wife. Nina with. . .

Francis
Everybody else I can relate to, but with your next door neighbor Nina?

Lillian
She should of have said no to crack!

Francis
She's on crack? I new something was wrong with her.

Lillian
Just me, my feeling for the old goat. Well, we all have problems.

Francis
I know, I shouldn't bring mine into the picture. Yours are probably far exceeding than mine.

Lillian
True.

Francis
I kind of thought that.

Lillian
(Changing the subject quickly). Well . . . Susan is a nice attractive girl . . You say she's a fantastic kisser, and she makes you feel different . . .Well how about asking her . . .

Francis
Whoa there Ms. Match Maker, I see where this is leading. Ma'ma I like Susan, but after Debbie, I'm not ready to plunge into another saga with another woman. *(Lillian is about to speak, Francis cuts her off).* Nice try I appreciate you looking after me and trying to make

things better.

Lillian
Well that's what mother's are for dear.

Francis
I love you. *(He kisses her on the cheek)*. We'll talk again about this later. But right now I better hit this book on remembering these lines. I can hear the voice of my Producer "If you don't get these lines down before the next taping of the show. . .Your ass is off the show!" Love you Ma'ma.

Lillian
and I love you Francis. *(He exits. The phone rings Lillian goes to answer it)*. Hello? Yes this is Lillian Bovell, who is this? Yvon from Dr. Lornborgs office . . Pardon? . . No . . .How about Wednesday? No dear, I'm afraid I'm all through with schedules and further treatments. You must be new. I'm past that stage now. Journey's end. Yes Dr. Van Lornborg discussed it with me... No dear it's all right, it's a part of life. Oh not here, I'll be spending those days, hopefully somewhere in the Caribbean or the Mediterranean. I'm looking somewhere tropical. Well it's been nice chatting with you, keep up the good work and tell the good Doctor, that Lillian sends her love. *(She hangs up the phone and the door bell rings, she wheels herself to answer the door)*. Eli come in.

Eli
Hello there. *(He takes off his hat)*, I was just thinking, I want to apologize for the trouble I've caused.

Lillian
Come in Eli, sit down. What trouble, with Nina? Listen the things she said about you and I, not to mention your divorce. It's not going to matter in a thousand years, besides in my opinion the old vulture deserved it.

Eli
I won't argue with you there. You know, when they made you they broke the mold.

Lillian
It was an accident. And now my warranty is expired.

86

Eli
You and your sister have the same type of humor.

Lillian
That we do. I was so surprised to see her up and walking.

Eli
She walked outside, she was amazed at the work I've done for you.
It was like it was her first time out in the garden.

Lillian
She doesn't get out much, but she's so wonderful, I love her to death,
I'm glad she is walking, up and about unlike me.

Eli
None of my business, but she asked me if you were having
chemotherapy.

Lillian
How did she find that out?

Eli
I believe she said by a phone call.

Lillian
Who did she call?

Eli
No one, the call came here from a Doctor's office. That's how she
knew.

Lillian
Well I can't hide it forever. Why should I, the phone call did come
from a Doctor's office and yes I am having chemotherapy, at least I
was.

Eli
Then you don't need the treatments anymore, You're healthy, right?

Lillian
(Beat). Sort of.

Eli
you're in remission?

Lillian
No. I'm going away, I'll be leaving. I'm going on a cruise, I'll send you a postcard.

Eli
Postcard. . . I understand. *(Pause. Making light of the subject).*
Have you decided what to wear on your cruise?

Lillian
Something outrageous and I'll bring lots of sun tan lotion with sun screen protection of 3000.

Eli
That would be you. You're good people, you and I have shared a few things in the past.

Lillian
That we have, not so easy working for a celebrity. Like when we got that write up in The Hollywood Informer by Nina.

Eli
Ah yes how could I forget.

Lillian
Eli, I just wanted to say, about this thing with me leaving.

Eli
Say no more, it's your way of dealing with it and it couldn't be a better idea. It's perfect.

Lillian
Thank you.

Eli
You know, Annie and I would watch you all the time, Annie loved the show. Wouldn't miss it for the world.

Lillian
Thank you, sure was fun, I wish I had made a come back, gone on forever.

Eli
I was wondering, how much does Audrey know. . .I mean about your condition?

Lillian
At this point just a phone call. Soon I'll have to tell her, not right now, things are gelling for her *(Beat)* and I want you to know something, just as an observation, I notice she comes alive where you are around.

Eli
You think so? Wait a minute, we were talking about you and then . .

Lillian
Listen she does come alive in your presence, don't you think that's great?

Eli
Yeah, Ok, so she comes alive, she's nice, funny. Attractive.

Lillian
Now you're talking.

Eli
Whoa, hold your horses lady. Are you playing some kind of personal Classified Ad here?

Lillian
Even if I am, it's harmless, I think you already like her.

Eli
Well I . . .Ok you got me. But. . .

Lillian
But nothing. You like her and you admitted it. And you haven't gone back to Annie. I don't think you will and to tell you the truth, she really wanted out.

Eli
You really think so?

Lillian
Of course, if she really loved you, she wouldn't let a stupid rumor bring on a divorce. No I believe it was an excuse. She had a significant other waiting to step into the picture.

Eli
More as I think about it you're absolutely right. But why are we talking about my life?

Lillian
Because it takes the focus off of mine. So about Audrey, she's nice, attractive and funny. Maybe a date, something could spark between you two.

Eli
Date? I can't imagine me dating. No can do.

Lillian
Oh humor a dying woman will ya.

Eli
Let me think about it. Well she does have those wonderful qualities about her, that we mentioned.

Lillian
See not all is lost she makes me laugh all the time, and lately her humor has been putting me to the test. I remember when I first came to San Francisco. Audrey joined me on New Years Eve and we went to this wonderful party, we had been drinking and laughing. Audrey and I were walking back to our room at the hotel. Audrey was wearing bright yellow pumps, don't know why, they didn't match her outfit and those yellow pumps didn't have a leather sole. That made the bottom of those shoes slippery. We were walking along, when out of the blue comes this gorgeous man to greet Audrey, he was too gorgeous, he must of been gay, I didn't tell Audrey that. He gave her a bundle of balloons and a big kiss on the cheek. Well she became all flustered. I went to help her, but I was noticed by a couple of fans so I signed autographs for them and when I turned back to look for Audrey, there she was rolling toward the bottom of the hill. All I could see were those bright yellow pumps, on and off, on and off, like a blinking hazzard light. I ran after her, but was too late, she hit a parking meter. So there I was, standing next to the meter and looking down at Audrey on the ground, I was having a good time., I was snockered. I put money in the meter and at the top of my lungs so everyone could hear, I said "She's parked for the night!" *(The laugh, it stops suddenly, when Susan and Antoine rush in).*

90

Lillian
Susan, Antoine, you're back early.

Susan
(Out of breath). Lil. . .

Lillian
What's the matter?

Antoine
(Out of breath). It's . . . I've got to catch my breath . . .

Lillian
It's what?

Susan
It's. . .

Lillian
(Charade like) Ok, sounds like? First word, first syllable of the
word.

Antoine
Audrey . . .

Eli
(Standing). What about Audrey. Where is she?

Susan
She, she, she, . .

Antoine
(Finally catching his breath). I got it from here.

Susan
Whew, thanks.

Lillian
Audrey, what about Audrey? Speak!

Antoine
She fell!!!

Lillian
NOOOOO!!!

(Black out)

End of Act 2, Scene 2

A few hours later.

(Lights Up, Lillian is playing her video game on the television, Antoine enters from the kitchen).

Antoine
(Sitting down on the edge of the sofa near Lillian). Hey you.

Lillian
Hello there.

Antoine
Whoa how far are you now?

Lillian
Don't know, I haven't been keeping track. How do you get passed that Fat Troll?

Antoine
(Raises and gives her instruction on the game). You have to give him a donut.

Lillian
OK I got the donut, how do I get him of my ass? He's tearing up my starship.

Antoine
Throw the donut out your ship's porthole. *(We hear a sound from the game then a burp sound).* There he got it. *(Beat).* How are you feeling today?

Lillian
Lousy as usual.

Antoine
Sorry.

Lillian
Oh no, here comes the troll again, I gave him the donut, now what? I won't be able to survive the next level.

Antoine
You have to give troll boy there a glazed donut, then pick up the red
pumps.

Lillian
What?

Antoine
(Pointing at the screen). There pick up the red pumps, so you can
boost your life span.

Lillian
Red pumps? I thought I needed to get the tiara first?

Antoine
You're not queen yet. First the red pumps then the tiara.

Lillian
Oh no, I can't get to them, I'm losing power.

Antoine
Right there, pick up that power source.

Lillian
I missed it, here come the cookies to eat me. I'm losing. My power
source is depleting.

Antoine
You're not gone yet, I'll bring you to the next level.

Lillian
It's no use I'm losing, I'm losing my life source *(Beat)*. I'm going to
die.

Antoine
Here let me help, I might be able to save you.

Lillian
Game over the giant cookies ate me all up. *(She puts game control
pad down and turns off the game).* I would have won, if that Fat Troll
didn't need a glazed donut!

Antoine
Sorry.

Lillian

I'll kick their butts next time. Oh I need to get out of this chair, I feel I'm getting a severe case of hemorrhoids.

Antoine

Want me to move you to the sofa?

Lillian

I'm doing ok for the present moment.

Antoine

(As he straightens her pillows in the chair and makes her comfortable). Your flowers are dying.

Lillian

That's a shame, we'll have to get more to take their place. How's Audrey?

Antoine

She's fine, but she's a little embarrassed, I would be too, she fell on the street in public. *(He throws the dead flowers away).*

Lillian

Poor dear, I should go see her.

Antoine

Lillian, I don't mean to bring this up, but you care to much about other people.

Lillian

What's wrong with that? I'll tell you something mister, I finally have a chance to do that now, I've been so busy the last ten years. I cared, but not as much as I should. Ooh, I think I need a pain pill now.

Antoine

I'll get one for you.

Lillian

That's all right sweetie, I have the good stuff in my room. Just give me a push. Thanks. *(He pushes Lillian to her room, a moment passes & Mason enters the livingroom, he is dressed in shorts and a tank top & stretches for his daily run, then he moves to the floor to do sit ups).*

Antoine
(Appearing as a wolf). Hmm, Hmm, Hello.

Mason
Hello, Antoine.

Antoine
Oh don't stop, I love to watch men work out, besides it'll be the thrill
of the day for me. Do you want me to hold your legs?

Mason
Pardon?

Antoine
To help do your sit-ups?

Mason
I'm fine.

Antoine
I'll say. *(Mason continues to do his sit-ups, Antoine continues to
stare).* You work out a lot?

Mason
Most of the time. I was a real Gym Rat, when I was with my Ex. He
wanted me in the gym 7 days a week. I wanted a relationship, he
wanted an Adonis. But I still stay in shape for myself.

Antoine
I see.

Mason
If you like, you can work out with me.

Antoine
Sure can I still hold your legs?

Mason
Naughty boy. Persistence will get you far.

Antoine
I know.

Mason
I have 10 more to go, then I'm done. *(He continues with his sit-ups)*. One, two, three, four. . .

Antoine
Slower, take your time.

Mason
If I do that, I'll loose momentum. Five...six...seven...*(Antoine tickles him)*. OK I'm done. *(Antoine rises, picks up a note book and proceeds to the desk, when a photo of him falls out of the note book)*. Thanks. . .*(He picks up the photo of Antoine)*. Here you dropped this, *(Takes a closer look at the photo)*. Is this you?

Antoine
(Not proud of the photo). Yeah. Doesn't look like me huh?

Mason
Sort of...You look sad in this picture.

Antoine
Sad? You're right. I don't know why I keep it. I was depressed a lot back then. I lost a lot of weight. It was the year I broke up with by Boyfriend, Paul, he was a loser, a heavy drinker. A few months later in that same year, I wasn't getting along well with my parents. My dad still had this thing about me, not really fitting in with the family, Once they knew, it threw a curve into our relationship. But I love my dad, and I know he loved me, well he wanted to talk, said it was time that we discussed things, be a family again, I'll call you, he said. But before we did that, I had to wait until he and mother got back from their vacation in Europe. I got the call, but it wasn't my father, it was some other man. . .Tragedy happened, the plane they were on went down. We never made the connection. . .I never had a chance to express my feelings to them. I guess this picture is all that I have, that reminds me of how I felt that day.

Mason
I'm terrible sorry, I didn't mean to pry.

Antoine
You're not prying. I can talk about it. It happened years ago. Listen, cutie, I believe there are people in this universe waiting to be born, to come down and journey through life on this planet. Like

96

you and me for instance, we are born, we make it through life as best as we know how, because we're here for this chain of events, that links up all together some how. This thing with my parents, that was part of my journey, I had to do through it to get to here.

Mason
How profound, are you sure you're not a writer?

Antoine
No, I'm a domestic in search of one.

Mason
Hmm.

Antoine
Can I ask you something? Why do you write?

Mason
It's what I like to do. Keeps me content. It certainly keeps my bills paid.

Antoine
Must be nice, I mean writing for one of the most watched daytime soaps on TV.

Mason
It's my job, and I love it. It challenges me all the time, to think up new plots and lines for the characters I create. Where can you write each week about, love, hate, deceit and foul play in the afternoon?

Antoine
All the good ingredients of a good soap opera.

Mason
Art imitates life.

Antoine
How come I've never met you sooner?

Mason
You weren't working for my mother last year were you?

Antoine
No, but I wish I had. *(Beat)*. Well enough about me. You have to get back to your writing.

Mason
You really like Ashley Steel?

Antoine
Yeah, she's one of my favorites to watch next to Francis. Ashley Steele, she's a true bitch until the end. It would be a shame to see her go. *(He exits)*.

Mason
(Sits, and at the desk, typing on his lap top computer, he chuckles thinking about the comment given by Antoine. Francis enters). Ok, Ashley Steele, you may survive after all . .

Francis
Oh it's you.

Mason
Who were you expecting, the Pope?

Francis
What are you working on?

Mason
The show.

Francis
Really.

Mason
I have some good ideas for Ashley Steele, for next weeks episode.

Francis
How about writing good ideas for my character.

Mason
What do you mean?

Francis
You know what the hell I mean. This business of writing that I'm in a hospital in New Delhi, with prostate trouble.

Mason
In that episode, we wrote that no Doctor in New Delhi had the knowledge to cure it. You had to be flown back here in the States to find out how to treat it.

Francis
Must be some stupid Doctors, who probably failed their urine exams!

Mason
You don't read the scripts. You have to let the dialogue flow.

Francis
Oh let the dialogue flow, listen to Tennessee Williams here without his bottle.

Mason
Shut up Francis, don't push me. I'll write your character having a more severe case of prostate problem and you will need Viagra to get it up! And how's this, then you're stuck in a Turkish prison. Later Mildred Princeton leaves you because you're this transsexual with red hair who looks for dates on the world wide web.

Francis
It could happen.

Mason
I'll make a note.

Francis
Go ahead you'll be on the streets looking for your next hand out.

Mason
Actors, you're all alike. Bunch of Prima Donnas.

Francis
Stop generalizing.

Mason
Ok. Only those actors in this room.

Francis
Do you know I make the ratings for this show?

Mason
Who do you think writes for this show so they will have the ratings?

Francis
They only see me.

Mason
But they hear me. My words.

Francis
My acting.

Mason
Oh! Puh-lease.

Francis
I rehearse all the time. We're always retaking scenes. Some of the
scenes I do live.

Mason
Goody, here's fifty cents. I hope you enjoy summer camp.

Francis
It would help if we had one script to follow, instead of several re-
written scripts.

Mason
Good point, I'll score one for you. Francis one, Mason Zip!

Francis
Why the hospital scene? Why couldn't you write Cameron in a
place, like a Romantic candle lit restaurant, a Honeymoon Suite at a
luxurious hotel, anywhere, but a hospital.

Mason
Sure, we'll place that whole operating scene in a restaurant, "Here
Doctor, this steak knife will have to do, excuse me Madame, but
are you using that salad fork? Don't mind us we're in a middle of a
Prostate surgery. Oh by the way how is the Prime Rib tonight?"

Francis
Smart Ass!

Mason
Scores one to one.

Francis
Here's one for you, your writing is way off from what it used to be.

Mason
Used to be? How would you know, you scene stealing hack.

Francis
That's it! *(He threw his finished pages onto the floor)>* I'm out of
here!

Mason
Very good. Now Francis I would like to be let alone so I can finish
my work!

Francis
In another part of the house! *(Throws more pages of the script onto
the floot).*

Mason
Francis what has gotten into you, are you on Vicadin?

Francis
Bite me!

Mason
I ought to slap you silly! *(They stand face to face as if to throw
punches).* Look at us, we're like a couple of vicious squirrels fighting
over an acorn nut! All right let's calm down. If you're that upset
about the scene I'll re-write it. The way you're acting, it seems
there's something else that's bothering you. Is it Debbie?

Francis
Debbie?

Mason
That girl you were seeing awhile back. You've been this way ever
since she left you for that baseball player, who owns that little café
on 16th and Fairfax.

Francis
At least he didn't have a prostate problem.

Mason
I said I'll work on it.

Francis
Five years we were together.

Mason
I know, but you cant' dwell on the past.

Francis
I know, she's out of my life. She's not what I'm concerned about.
It's something else.

Mason
What do you mean something else?

Francis
I think Ma'ma is much more ill, than she appears to be.

Mason
You think so?

Francis
Yeah.

Mason
Maybe she's sick from the last time.

Francis
No it's more serious I think.

Mason
Are you sure? The last time she had a mild case, swollen hands, feet,
not to mention the awful diarrhea she had. I mean we all can get it.

Francis
How could she get it twice and still be sick?

Mason
I did, when I used to eat off those lunch wagon trucks at work.

Francis
Is that what happened when you took time from work? You used
vacation time for that?

Mason
Yeah. Warning, don't eat their egg salad sandwiches.

Francis
It just seems to me she looks different, more frail than the last time
when we visited.

Mason
You're right she does look more frail.

Francis
I don't want to jump to conclusions here and upset her.

Mason
No, not a good idea.

Francis
I'll find out, I'm sure she'll tell me.

Mason
Sure she will.

Francis
Well maybe, if it's serious, you know she won't say a thing, she's good a keeping secrets.

Mason
That's for sure.

Francis
Sorry I knocked your papers onto the floor and yelled at you.

Mason
I forgive you. Listen things will balance out. (*He closes his lap top computer and starts to leave the room*).

Francis
Wait, Next week's show, am I out of the hospital?

Mason
If you're real nice to me, I'll write that you get out of the hospital and let laid.

Francis
I'm nice, I'm nice. (*Mason ascends upstairs. Susan enters from the front door carrying a bag of groceries, she accidentally drops the bag*).

Susan
Oh heck! Antoine help!

Francis
Susan I think he's gone out. Here let me get that for you.

Susan
I should of told them to give me plastic. Are the eggs broken?

Francis
(Looking in the bag to check). They're fine, none broken.

Susan
Thank you, for a moment I thought I had to go back to the store.

Francis
You need help carrying those bags to the kitchen?

Susan
There not that heavy, I can get them.

Francis
Susan, can I ask you something, you know seeing my mother, she seems frail. How long has she been sick?

Susan
(Covering). For awhile now, fractured hips they can take a long time to heal, and they can make the person look frail, because they don't get around much and they don't eat . . *(Looking inside the bag)*. Oh I do have to go back to the store, I forgot to get coffee.

Francis
Mind if I tag along?

Susan
I would love to have you... I mean, yes please tag along. I might need some help to pick things off the aisle floors for me. *(They exit together. Lillian enters and she wheels herself towards the kitchen, the phone rings stopping to answer it)*.

Lillian
Hello, yes this is Lillian . . .Who? . . Eddie!. . .it's good to hear from you . . I'm doing the best that I can. . .Why thank you. I need all the prayers I can get. No, I decided to spend those days somewhere else... I'll send you a postcard, is Tracy still there? I miss him doing my make-up, and our little espresso chats together...Oh is that right, Rosemary is head of production now, wow ...Her husband Ron has moved into the director's chair? ...Clare our dear Clare, is an executive producer? . . What's that? . . . Carolyn is head stage manager. . .What about Mr. Boisvert? He's head designer for the show? . . my, my, I have been away too long. *(Audrey peers in and listens but unseen by Lillian)*. Oh . . You're busy again, calling

between takes huh? Ok Eddie, tell everyone I send my love and that I miss CBS. Take care sweetie*(She hangs up the phone)*. Audrey . .

Audrey
(Standing tall and walking boldly).

You and I have to talk.

Lillian
Uh oh.

Audrey
How long do you think you could hide it?

Lillian
Hide what dear?

Audrey
All right. To the point. I know you're ill, very ill. I know about the cancer.

Lillian
Cancer?

Audrey
Cut the act Lil. How long do you think you could keep your little secret. I called I found out the hard way. Who else have you hidden this from?

Lillian
Just about everyone. I am sure they'll find out.

Audrey
My God, why didn't you say anything? Why, Lil. Why? Especially to me, your own sister. I'm always the last to know!

Lillian
I would have . . . in time.

Audrey
When? When it's too late?

Lillian
Audrey, I don't want everyone worrying about me. You have your own problems. Your foot, the cat needing to be fixed, the roaches.

Audrey
Little problems, don't play the martyr. It won't work.

Lillian
Audrey, I just want everyone to be happy. I don't want them worrying about some dying woman. I've lived my life. I'm through. I'm just waiting for my exit line.

Audrey
What are you talking about, "Everyone to be Happy?" You don't make any sense.

Lillian
You're right, I don't make sense, *(Beat)*. And I do have cancer. Terrible of me not to mention it. I'm sorry.

Audrey
Why did you hide it?

Lillian
The reason is I have about six months left, if that, to fulfil those remaining days I have left. No need to worry about my estate, I have taken care of all the duties of my house and other loose ends. I want everyone to be happy.

Audrey
Happy that you're dying? What kind of sick joke is that?

Lillian
Audrey get on with your life. Start over where you left off.

Audrey
Start over? How can I? I'm losing my sister. I'm never going to see you again! How can you say start over and be happy? I'll be more screwed up than before.

Lillian
You're not screwed up, you only think that you are. You can start over. People start over with their lives all the time.

Audrey
Oh like I'm going to attend some kind of cancer survival start over again group, in back of some coffee shop to help me get through this and start over.

Lillian
Yeah, maybe you can start on meeting on Wednesdays.

Audrey
It's not funny, you have a joke for everything.

Lillian
That's what keeps me sane. And I will let you in on something, I certainly do not want to die in a hospital bed with tubes stuck in my body and hooked up to some machine to keep me alive. With no one coming to visit me, because they don't want to see me that way and when I do go, more than likely, the only thought is, when all my friends and family are at my funeral, is the last vision they will remember me, is in that casket. I can hear the dialogue now, "She looked good. She looked like she was asleep, so peaceful, they did a nice job on her make-up" I say to that, Bullshit! I'm going to finish my journey on a tropical cruise. Audrey it's a better way of saying good bye. I'm doing it for me and the ones I love. Do you understand?

Audrey
(Pause). Yes, I understand.

Lillian
Then show me you do, because I don't have time to sit here and argue with you over what I did wrong. Start over, live again. See life in a different perspective. Be alive. Life is full of amazement, with every turn, there is something wonderful to discover. *(Pause)*. Make the most of your journey through this life.

Audrey
How damn it?

Lillian
I don't know how, that's up to you, I don't have all the answers.

Audrey
If you don't have all the answers, then I'm sure someone else does, where is everyone?

Lillian
Francis is probably studying his lines with Susan . . . Maybe. And I think, Mason and Antoine are spending time together. . . I hope.

Audrey
How can you be so calm about all this?

Lillian
It's a talent, Audrey I love you and I wouldn't do anything to hurt you. I'm terribly sorry I didn't tell you sooner and about you not having the answers, I believe you already know the answers, you just need some guidance.

Audrey
Lillian, sometimes you amaze me.

Lillian
I amaze myself. . .*(She has pain)*. If you will excuse me dear, I need to take another pill. *(The door bell rings)*. I wonder who that can be. Audrey dear could you get the door please, thank you.

(She exits to down stairs restroom).

Audrey
(She wheels Lillian to the restroom then pulls herself together, before she answers the door).

Hello there Eli.

Eli
Hello there Audrey, how's the foot?

Audrey
It's doing much better.

Eli
Glad to hear it. The nursery gave me extra Violets, care to take them home with you to plant in your yard?

Audrey
How nice, thank you.

Eli
You seem down about something. Is Nina's dog back? Why I oughta . . .

Audrey
No, Lillian and I were chatting about something.

Eli
Is everything all right? Are you OK?

Audrey
At this moment I don't know. So much to absorb right now.

Eli
I understand. . . Would you also like to take some Gladiolas, I have tons of them that you might want to plant at your house.

Audrey
I like Gladiolas, one of my favorite flowers. But I don't know what to do with them, maybe all those chemicals the exterminators used will kill my flowers.

Eli
Don't worry pesticides only work on pests.

Audrey
That's good to know. At this point I need to go to my house, check on things.

Eli
If you need a ride, I'll be glad to load up those Gladiolas and away we'll go.

Audrey
That's nice of you, I need someone to talk to.

Eli
Where do you live?

Audrey
Just over the Golden Gate Bridge. *(They exit out the front door a moment passes, then Antoine enters from the front door we hear some words of exchange as he had passed Audrey and Eli. Slamming his day planner on the u.s. table, reading a note then rips it up).*

Antoine
I could never fall in love with you. Bullshit! But you can love everyone else! *(Lillian enters).*

Lillian
Upset about something dear?

Antoine

Victor! He wanted to talk to me, so we met at the Patio Café on the Castro. He seemed nice. He wines and dines me and there we are having a pleasant conversation. Then after we finish, this lovely meal, he gives me this letter! *(He reads the letter).* "I don't think I can fall in love with you. We have nothing common. I hope you don't take this the wrong way." How am I supposed to take this? Lying down! He thinks he can't fall in love with me. Bullshit, he loves everyone else: Joey, Bobby, Mark, Tom, Dick and Harry! And I don't even know them!

Lillian

Why do you put up with that?

Antoine

I must be a glutton for punishment!

Lillian

He's not worth it.

Antoine

You're right, he's not. I need to go shopping.

Lillian

Well hang in there dear, things get better with time. *(She goes to the desk).* I have something here that will cheer you up. *(Handing him an envelope).*

Antoine

(Opening the envelope). Two tickets to Les Miserable. Who am I going to ask to go with me, Victor? Hello, I don't think so.

Lillian

No, not Victor.

Antoine

When would you like to go?

Lillian

Not me, I saw it, great show. Especially the actor who plays Jon Val John. I was thinking of the idea of Mason going with you.

Antoine

You think he would?

110

Lillian
Maybe if you ask him.

Antoine
I see your wings clicking together cupid . . I like it!

Lillian
I thought you would.

Antoine
Thank you, Lillian you're the best person I have ever worked for, ever. I never worked for someone who cares so much as you do. I'm not just saying that to make you feel good. Believe me, if I could make you feel better I would. Something else I would want to say, you've been like a mother to me and I don't want to see you go. Sorry I didn't mean to bring that up. You have the best damn Cruise there is, and take lots of pictures.

Lillian
You bet I will buster. *(She looks about the room).* By the way have you seen Audrey?

Antoine
Oh, I forgot to tell you I got side tracked with Victor getting me all upset. I passed Audrey and Eli, outside, they were on their way to her house.

Lillian
Did she say what for?

Antoine
She didn't say.

Lillian
Hmm, I just wonder if she was upset with me for telling her about my condition.

Antoine
You told her, how did she take it?

Lillian
Relatively well, I think.

Antoine
Have you told your sons yet?

Lillian
No, but I believe Francis knows.

Antoine
In my opinion you should tell them.

Lillian
Yes you're right, I'm having a tough time doing it. When the time is right I need to tell them.*(She has more discomfort)*. Oh La, la. . .Oh! If you'll excuse me sweetie I believe the bathroom is calling me.

Antoine
Are you OK?

Lillian
Just help me to the door, I need a head start. Push on the chair easy, but fast . . .Hurry!

(He helps her to the down stairs bathroom, then Mason enters reading the changes he has made in the show's script).

Antoine
Hi.

Mason
Hi, well she's back in.

Antoine
Who's back in?

Mason
I thought about what you said and I decided to put Ashley Steele back into the picture.

Antoine
She's back in? The bitch lives! Yeah she's alive again! Cool, can I read the script?

Mason
Not just yet, I have some more work to do with her, still working how she comes back alive from the accident when she was on that African Safari hunt with the Rhinos. *(He grabs the door handle to*

the downstairs bathroom and juggles it).

Lillian
(From inside the bathroom). Hello?

Antoine
Lillian is in there.

Mason
Sorry Ma'ma.

Antoine
Mason, have you ever seen Les Miserable?

Mason
Yes I have.

Antoine
(Disappointed). Oh.

Mason
Why?

Antoine
I just thought you might like to go, I have two tickets for tomorrow
night.

Mason
I'd love to. I wouldn't mind seeing it again.

Antoine
Really?

Mason
I love the part of Jon Val John, the actor who plays that part is
wonderful!

Antoine
So I've heard.

Mason
Oh I shouldn't say anything about it, don't want to give it away. Are
the tickets for tonight?

Antoine
No, there for tomorrow night.

Mason
Great. In the meantime I need a break from my writing. Do you like Chinese?

Antoine
Men?

Mason
Food.

Antoine
Yeah right. I love Chinese. I know a fabulous restaurant we could go to just down the street from here.

Mason
Excellent. *(Lillian exits from the downstairs bathroom)*. Ma'ma how would you like to join Antoine and I for Chinese?

Lillian
I don't think I'm up to it. Besides I'll be in the way.

Mason
We can't leave you here alone. We'll have it delivered.

Lillian
That's all right, Susan should be back shortly. I'm just not up to eating.

Mason
I know what it is, I should get you some Imoduim AD.

Lillian
Would you go. Have fun. Here take the car. Well go on. The Mercedes has gas. *(Beat)*.

What are you expecting a Peugeot?

Mason
I promise, we won't be gone long.

Lillian
For crying out loud, stop worrying about me and go.

Mason
(Kissing her on the cheek). Bye. *(Whispering).* He's so cute.

Antoine
Be right back. *(He gives her a kiss on the cheek).* He's very
handsome, I love the glasses, makes him look very distinguished. If
only Victor could see me now.

Lillian
Bye you two have fun.

*(They exit out the front door, then a moment passes then we hear the
voices of Mason, Antoine and Susan as the pass each other outside.
Susan enters).*

Lillian
There she is.

Susan
I know that look on your face, sorry I'm late.

Lillian
Where were you?

Susan
I was with Francis, we went to get coffee. I had to go back to the
store to get it. I picked out your favorite kind, French Vanilla Roast.

Lillian
All is forgiven, where is Francis?

Susan
He got a call. He's outside on his cell phone talking to his agent.

Lillian
That figures. *(Susan in a down mood).* What's the matter dear?

Susan
Nothing is the matter, in fact everything is going great.

Lillian
Do tell.

Susan
I'm having a great time with knowing Francis, he's funny, he's handsome, charming, he's all those things, pardon me, but he turns me on. . .a great deal.

Lillian
All that from just getting coffee?

Susan
He's what I like in a man, there's no one like him and he likes me . . .me, but he's a celebrity and I'm just a working class girl.

Lillian
What a way to think of yourself, stop talking like that.

Susan
I seem so average.

Lillian
Stick a sock in it girl, you're an attractive and intelligent girl, obviously Francis knows you.

Susan
Francis is certainly different from the guy I was with Rick Burly, more like, Mr, Liar dot COM. And how can I be thinking of men, when I should be doing my job of taking care of you?

Lillian
I'm not complaining and I have everything packed and I'm ready to go. Susan you have done a tremendous job of taking care of me. It's your time now. Enjoy getting to know Francis.

Susan
I'm going to miss you. *(They hug, then Francis appears, Susan spots him)*. Francis . . .We didn't hear you come in.

Francis
I knew I was right when I told Mason there was more to your illness, than meets the eye. No need to explain Susan told me.

Susan
I'm so sorry Lillian.

Lillian
It's OK honey.

Francis
I'm not upset with you, it's just that sometimes I don't understand why. Of course, I've never understood anything in this family, but that doesn't matter now. I believe you're doing the right thin, and I support you.

Lillian
Francis please, I meant to explain, but I'm afraid I did a poor job of it. Forgive me.

Francis
I forgive you. I love you, you're such a bold woman. I'm aware of what is about to happen. I know what my feelings are, but at this moment, I need sometime to think about how I'm going to say goodbye. *(He exits out the French doors)*.

Lillian
Francis don't go, Francis! *(The door bell rings)*. Damn these interruptions!

Susan
I'll get it.

(She goes to answer the door). Hello Nina.

Nina
Hello Susan.

Lillian
Hello Nina, what brings you out into the sunlight?

Nina
I just wanted to let you know, that my little paper likes you.

Lillian
What do you mean?

Nina
You know what I mean . . *(Something catches her eye as she passes by the French doors)*. Hello.

Lillian
Who are you waving at?

Nina
Audrey your sister. She is your sister isn't she?

Lillian
(To Susan who now sees Audrey up in a tree). Of course she's my
sister. . . Audrey's outside?

Susan
Outside up in a tree.

Lillian
What?

Nina
That's interesting, your sister up in a tree, now what could she be
doing there, Hmm?

Susan
(Covering). She's picking walnuts.

Nina
(Looking outside at Audrey in the tree). She's the biggest one I know.
In fact the whole family has gone Fruit Loop.

Lillian
She's always climbing tree's, rocks, buildings and she's in training,
so she can get ready to go on that mountain climbing trip of hers
next week. Audrey, it's time to come down dear. Stop showing off!

Audrey
(From outside in the tree). Not yet, the view is marvelous, you can
see all of San Francisco up here.

Lillian
I'm sure you can, come on down, how about a break, have a power
bar.

Nina
this could make a lovely story.

Lillian
What are we going to do?

Susan
I know, do you have a banana?

Lillian
No, would a bb gun work?

Nina
(Pulling out a note pad to jot down some notes for her story). OK,
let's see, sister up in tree . . She thinks she's a bird, no a monkey . .
.Yeah thinks she's a monkey. . .

Susan
Nina don't you dare!

Nina
And what is Eli going at the bottom of the tree with pruning sheers,
could be foul play.

Susan
Audrey, Please come down!

Audrey
Lillian, I'm awake, you're absolutely right I need to go on with my
Life!

Nina
What did she say? Did she say you and her had a fight? I'll have to
write that down.

Lillian
Nina, there's no need to do this. It's me you want, not her, leave my
sister out of this.

Nina
Oh tsh, tsh, Audrey why are you up in that tree? Is it true that
eating a walnut changed your life, and made you high as a kite.
And you think you are a monkey with wings or is it really that
you're adopted, and none of the family cares for you and if Humpty
Dumpty Audrey falls there will be no one to catch her.

Lillian
Get her away from the door! *(Eli enters carrying Pruning Sheers)*.
Eli, Eli please help Audrey down out of the tree.

119

Eli

She's all right don't worry, I'll get her down. I was pruning those branches earlier, I guess she climbed up there and the ladder fell.

Nina

I could use that too. Adoptee, stuck in a backyard tree. . .

Eli

Nina mind your own business and stay out of theirs, before you ruin these peoples lives!

Nina

Are those pruning sheers? Did you threaten Audrey with those? That's why she's stuck in the tree. I see it now. Crippled sister scared to death, drags herself out of the house. Climbs up a tree. Threatening gardener, who wants to prune more that the trees. Family doesn't care, because she is adopted. This will make a fine story.

Eli

You bitch!

Nina

I know. I better get started. *(She writes more down in her note pad).*

Eli

Don't you ever give up?

Nina

I never give up, not when there is a good story to write about. This one's for my Edsel, My precious. The one that was accused of drop and run.

(Francis enters, the Eli exits to Audrey out of the tree).

Francis

Ma'ma I wanted to say that . . .

Nina

Oh my gosh, it's him, it's you, oh my! At last we meet.

Susan

Francis, it's the next door gossip whore. Remember?

120

Francis
Oh yeah that one. I'll take care of it. Hello there, you must be Ms. Chadwell.

Nina
Call me Nina.

Francis
(Playing the act). Nina, Nice name Nina and sexy too.

Nina
Sexy, I like sexy, tell me more about sexy. But slowly.

Francis
Sure.

Nina
Say are you up for an interview. I have my pen and pad ready?

Francis
Whatever you got, I'm ready, come on over here so that we can talk.

Nina
I'm right behind ya stud.

(They move away from the others, Francis gives them a look as if I can handle this one. He gives the others a wink. Eli enters carrying Audrey, he sets her down on the sofa).

Audrey
You're a strong man, thank you Eli.

Eli
There you go Audrey, I apologize for the ladder falling.

Audrey
Silly of me to think I'm a kid again, climbing trees.

Eli
But it was worth it, Great view huh?

Audrey
It sure is. How do you stay pleasant all the time?

Eli
The only way I can answer that is: Where there is a weed, there is a flower. Life isn't all grim, life isn't all weeds.

Audrey
Huh?

Eli
Never mind.

Audrey
You're beginning to grow on me like vine Eli.

Eli
I was kind of hoping . . .Lillian she seems to be all right. I'd better put that ladder away.

Lillian
Good idea. *(To Eli)*. I'm not too old to spot love.

Eli
Must be those eagle eyes of yours. *(He winks, he steps out through the French doors)*.

Francis
I'm glad we had this little chat.

Nina
Me too, Thank you for the picture. Sexy . . .

Francis
(Gives her a wink). Your welcome Nina.

Lillian
Nina, you're not going to write that story are you?

Nina
Story, what story? Look at this face, those eyes, those lips. Who spoke to me and said the word sexy/ *(She exits out the front door)*.

Lillian
Thank you son.

Susan
What did you do? She was like in a daze.

Francis
I just charmed the old medusa.

Susan
To a drooling state.

Francis
I decided we need to stay, and see you off on your . . .cruise.

Lillian
I love you son *(They hug)*. Now you two scuttle outside to talk, I need a moment with Audrey.

Susan
(Playing). If we may, could I see you outside in the garden.

Francis
So that we can talk. *(They exit out to the garden)*.

Lillian
Audrey you had me worried.

Audrey
I'm sorry Lillian, I just wasn't thinking. Eli and I were about to drive to my house. But we decided to stay outside, it's so pretty, and relaxing. It got me talking. Eli and I talked about life, then I told him about you and everything, but he already knew. Then he cheered me up by reciting some of his bad poetry about composting. He does have a wonderful heart and he's attractive, easy going man. We had a nice time talking. I like him.

Lillian
How wonderful, see things will be fine.

Audrey
I hope they will.

Lillian
Audrey, do yourself a favor, go bra-less, it takes away the wrinkles.

Audrey
I wish it was that easy.

Lillian

Don't hold back, because of me. I haven't seen you this happy in a long time. Be good to yourself, you deserve it. Let's celebrate, I'll get a nice Merlot and we'll all meet outside in the garden.

Audrey

OK. Lillian I must say I'm learning a lot from you. I think for the first time, I'm seeing things from a different angle. *(She exits the garden as Lillian gets wine from the rack U.S.R. Meanwhile Mason & Antoine have returned).*

Lillian

It's what makes this human experience so wonderful, keep that going dear sister and you'll be fine.

Antoine

Hello, we're back.

Mason

We bought enough for everyone.

Lillian

Great. Everyone is out back I believe discovering wisdom. We were just about to celebrate.

Mason

Celebrate what?

Lillian

Life . . .My life, your life. You like Merlot?

Mason

Sure.

Antoine

I'll get wine glasses. *(He exits to the kitchen).*

Lillian

I'm so glad to see you two getting to know each other. You two look happy together. I think you make a wonderful couple.

Mason

You're too much for words.

Lillian
As long as they're not four letter words. Time to celebrate. *(Beat).*
You know, I'm gonna miss all of this.

Mason
We'll miss more that . . .

Antoine
I better see if the others want food. *(He exits out the French doors).*

Mason
Ma'ma I know.

Lillian
About me? My condition? I figured you would. Family secrets what
a shame they are. Afraid the world will know.

Mason
Francis told me.

Lillian
How's he doing?

Mason
Coping just like me.

Lillian
I'm a terrible mother.

Mason
Not in the least. I wish you would have told us earlier, that's the
terrible part. There has been some surprises, since we came. It's
something you didn't want to broadcast, I know I can relate. *(He
starts to cry).* I'm sorry, I told myself to be strong, I did not want to
do this.

(Pause).

Lillian
It's going to be OK son.

Mason
How are we going to get along without you?

Lillian

Just fine. You're a writer. Talk about me, write about me. Make me one of your characters. It will be good therapy for you.

Mason

As I look at you, listen to you, why is it that I'm talking a course in Psyche 101.

Lillian

Because I already took the course. Now chin up, lets eat spend time with me, before I go.

Mason

(Making light of the subject(. So where have you decided to go?

Lillian

Well I thought about Greece, I always wanted to see MT. Olympus. Visit with Zeus and all the other Gods. But I've come to the conclusion, that I will be in the French Riviera. Get a chance to see some of the talented artists at work and maybe a film or two, at the Cannes.

Mason

Well then, let's eat, drink and start the festivities.

Lillian

That's the spirit.

Mason

I'll get the others. *(He exits out the French doors, Lillian wheels herself to follow, then a sharp pain hit her suddenly. She reaches out toward the doors, then the pain stops she realizes, it's time to go. She grabs her sun glasses and her summer outrageous hat. Phone rings and she goes to answer it).*

Lillian

Hello? . . . This is Lillian. . . Yes, I sent for the limo. I believe it's time for me. It's on it's way. It'll be here any minute, thank you.

(Mason re-enters with others, she has hold of her sun glasses and hat she has another moment of pain).

Mason

Ma'ma . . . *(He goes to her).*

126

Audrey
Lil.

Lillian
It's time for me to be going, I can't stay too long. The limo is coming to get me. Let's have that glass of Merlot.

(She has a slight pain again).

Francis
Ma'ma are you all right?

Susan
I'll get your pills.

Mason
Want us to move you to your room?

Eli
That's a good idea.

Antoine
I'll get you a glass of water.

Lillian
Stop all of you. I'm fine. I just drifted off a little that's all.

Audrey
Maybe you should rest awhile.

Lillian
I do need that, but my ride will be here soon to take me to the airport.

Audrey
(Pours the wine for all). Here is your Merlot Lil.

Lillian
Thank you Audrey. Here's to each and everyone of you, I truely want to say, thank you all for being there for me. It has been a great pleasure knowing you. Here's to life and may your life's jouney be a fulfilling one. Cheers!

All
Cheers!

Susan
(Susan looks out the window and spots the Limo). Your limo is here.

Lillian
Sooner than I expected. *(Another sharp pain).* Ohh! Well My
Denouement, *(Mason & Francis move to each side of her wheelchair).*
You two are such fine angels, would you be so kind to escort me to
my chariot. *(She turns and gives a big kiss goodbye and puts on her
hat and sun glasses).* Oh by the way is the hat a little too much?

Antoine
Perfect honey.

Lillian
(She turns to the others and blows a kiss goodbye). Bon voyage.

All

Bon Voyage *(Lillian exits out the others follow her to the door).*

(Lights slowly fade out)

*What we had just witnessed was unfolding of a soap opera show, "As
the Evening Falls"*

*lights come back up to full, and the voice of an announcer is heard
over a mic sound system.*

Announcer's voice:

As the Evening Falls was brought to you by Clelestrol. A sure way
to lose inches from you waist, a medicated use for those wanting
to reach their ideal weight. Common side effects are, Sore throat,
muscle and joint discomfort, vomiting, loss of hair and a mild case of
explosive diarrhea.

(Then the voice of a director's voice is heard).

Director's voice:

Alright everyone that's a Rap!

(Then technicians carrying cameras, clipboards, cable cords etc. etc. Then one by one the actors come out as to get ready to go home. The next given dialogue maybe expressed by the actors, by using their real names i.e. good work Bob, goodnight Ruth, etc. etc. Fantastic job everyone! Check your schedule before you go home tonight. This next segment should be used as a curtain call for the actors which they themselves call each other by their real names.)

Nina
(Taking off her wig). This thing is hot, glad to get this off. *(To the other actor)*. Did we miss any lines *(Addressing actor's real name)*. _____?

Eli
No I don't think so, and if we did, we would have notes tonight. I'm ready for the rap party.

How about you?

Nina
Totally.

Susan
(Coming back on stage). Wow what a show huh guys?

Audrey
(Entering). Hey everybody we did it. Where's the party? Hey listen, could you walk me to my car? *(Exits)*.

Susan
I'll walk you to your car*(Actors real name)*._____ do you know the way to Sid's house? For the party? There's a map posted in the green room, but if you want, why don't you ride with me?

Audrey
OK let me get my things, meet you around back *(They exit out)*.

Francis
(Entering- Actor's real name)._____are you joining us tonight?

Mason
What are you kidding? I wouldn't miss this in a life time. I'll catch up to you, let me get my coat.

Francis
All right I'll see if one of the girls need a ride. *(He exits out).*

Antoine
(To Mason as the actor). Your mother would be very happy with the show, if she were here today.

Mason
(Pause). The look on her face. She would be very happy to have seen this show.

(The two exit out together)

(Finally Lillian enters)

Lillian
My butt is sore, more padding next time in that chair. Sid does Lillian come back for another episode?

Director's Voice:

Isn't she on vacation? Will discuss that with the writers.

Lillian
OK I'll get my things and see you at the rap party! *(She waves out into the audience).* Night everyone, hope you had a good time. *(She exits a lonely spotlight fades out on a picture of Lillian, as the Song by Nat King Cole, "Unforgettable" chimes in)*

THE END

About the Author

D.M. Schuetteé has taken us down the run way of a fashion show, from his play "Positively Entertaining" Where the clothing designer is color blind, and the models are everything from dieting, hot flashes to obsessive compulsive disorders. Now he takes us inside the home of Lillian Bovell, a retired talk show host whose life revolves around her live -in assistants, and her forty five-year-old needy sister Audrey that has to have her cat cheeto neutered. If that isn't enough, she gets a surprise visit from her two sons in the middle of the night, upsetting the household to chaotic stress. While the next door neighbor Nina a newspaper reporter spying in on their every move to get all the juicy details of a top story. As the plot thickens, Lillian has a secret that soon all will be revealed which brings "Love, Hate, Deceit and Foul Play in the Afternoon".

Printed in the United States
37617LVS00006B/361-363